Humbled
— on —
Purpose

DISCOVERING STRENGTH
THROUGH VULNERABILITY
HUMOR AND GRACE

Humbled
— ON —
Purpose

Maggie Michaels DeCan

Ripples Media

"It has been a distinct privilege to work with Maggie DeCan for over a decade, first and foremost as a friend, but also through the Children's Development Academy. She has been a serious business and professional leader of the school, both through fun and prosperous times as well as challenging times, including navigating COVID, which require both heart and clarity of mind to make difficult decisions. *Humbled on Purpose* manages to seamlessly weave valuable career guidance with honest, heartfelt personal reflection in a remarkably moving and joyful story."

Joseph B. Alonso
Founder of Alonso & Wirth and Former Board Chair of Children's Development Academy

"Humility and success don't always go together. It takes a remarkable person to have both. Maggie tells her story in a witty, humorous way that draws you in and inspires you. Everyone has a story to tell; but not everyone can tell it as well as Maggie does in this book."

Sherri Harris
Owner and CEO of Staff Zone, Harris Investment Holdings, LLC and Select People Inc.

"Hearing Maggie share how she took a humbling situation and allowed herself permission to continue her leadership journey in a new direction, focused on her personal passion rather than a big salary, is incredibly moving. I've witnessed her leadership, excellence, and friendship since the day we met at Michigan. Maggie's always been a skilled leader, and, through her experiences, speaks to the truths of how to transition your career by leading with honesty and authenticity."

Carole Widmayer
CEO of The Coffee Cherry Co.

"It is not often that the human soul gives itself permission to be vulnerable, transparent, and raw, exposing the innermost thoughts with gripping humility and truth. That's what this book does! DeCan writes in a witty and authentic way, brilliantly sharing the trials and triumphs that we can model and learn from."

Dr. Dawn Marie Kier
Chief Heart Doctor at New Dawn Consulting, Board Member Family Promise, Pastor, and certified Executive Coactive Coach

"*Humbled on Purpose* is the perfect combination of storytelling and career guidance. As a person on my own professional journey, reading about how Maggie overcame significant personal and professional obstacles on her path to success is inspiring. Her wisdom on topics ranging from navigating workplace dynamics to how to identify and advance your own career goals is invaluable. Finding true professional fulfillment is elusive to most, but Maggie has definitely found it. I hope to use the lessons in her book to find my own 'CDA.'"

Lauren Trant
Family law attorney, Kaye, Lembeck, Hitt & French

"Over the past twenty years, I have experienced exponential personal growth that stemmed from my time with a few great leaders. Maggie challenged me to get a degree and, at the age of fifty-two, I accomplished something I never thought achievable. The learnings from that experience led me to a successful career in Human Resources. When Maggie left the organization to run a non-profit there was something missing in the lives of those she touched. I know she will continue to influence leaders at all levels in the next chapter."

Cindy Sutton
CDA Board Member, Retired Vice President of Operations, The HoneyBaked Ham Company

"Leaders are not created in Business School, they are created through the learnings that come from failures and successes. In *Humbled on Purpose*, Maggie describes overcoming huge personal challenges that would have limited the success and happiness of most people. Instead, she focused on achievement, recognizing the talents others bring, and continually adapting to new opportunities to achieve personal and organizational results thought unattainable in both for-profit and non-profit companies. Read this book and learn about Radical Gratitude."

Doug Higgins
Metro Atlanta President of United Community Bank and Board Member of the Children's Development Academy

"Maggie's memoir is remarkable in its candor, inspiration, grief, and ultimately, triumph. It's not possible to read this book and be unchanged or unmoved by the experience."

John Ray
Business Advisor and Author, *The Generosity Mindset*

Published by Ripples Media
www.ripples.media

Copyright © 2024 by Maggie Michaels DeCan

All rights reserved. No part of this book may be reproduced or used in any manner without written permission of the copyright owner except for the use of quotations in a book review. For more information: contact@ripples.media

First printing 2024

Book and cover designed by Burtch Hunter

ISBN 979-8-9914473-0-0 Paperback
ISBN 979-8-9914473-1-7 Hardback
ISBN 979-8-9914473-2-4 E-book

To Bob, Riley and Brady.
Thank you or letting me share
some of our embarrassing but true, funny stories
with strangers in the spirit of helping others
along the way.
It's what we do now. I love you.

CONTENTS

FOREWORD xi

CHAPTER 1
FIGHTING FOR A (MASSIVE) PAY CUT 1

CHAPTER 2
LIFE IS SHORT (MINE WAS UNFAIR EARLY) 17

CHAPTER 3
HAIL TO THE VICTORS, LEADERS AND BEST (YEARS) 35

CHAPTER 4
THE PERFECT(LY AWFUL) MANAGER 47

CHAPTER 5
(SCAR-BASED) LEADERSHIP 67

CHAPTER 6
THE CDA'S FIRST HARD YEAR (DITCH OF DESPAIR) 91

CHAPTER 7
SEE CHANGES 125

CHAPTER 8
WHY THE CDA? 143

CHAPTER 9
GOOD COMPANY(IES) 157

CHAPTER 10
THE BIG PICTURE 167

EPILOGUE 175
EXPRESSIONS OF RADICAL GRATITUDE 179
ABOUT THE AUTHOR 185

FOREWORD

I'M THRILLED to write this foreword for my dear friend Maggie. She and I have been friends for years, brought together by our sons, who've been close friends since sixth grade. Over the years, our little group of moms has shared countless Wednesday meet-ups, where we'd catch up on life, laugh a lot, and support each other through all the ups and downs.

It was during these times that I had the privilege of hearing about Maggie's incredible journey from her high-powered role in the corporate world, to taking on a new challenge leading the Children's Development Academy (CDA), a nonprofit preschool program for those whose families otherwise couldn't afford it. I watched as Maggie navigated this transition with grace and determination. She didn't just step into the nonprofit world—she brought all her experience, energy, and a touch of that Maggie magic to the CDA, transforming it into something truly special. The impact she made there is a legacy that will last for years to come.

What always struck me was how Maggie managed to balance everything with such humility. She took the challenges head-on, never losing sight of her purpose. It wasn't always easy, but Maggie showed us all what it means to lead with heart, to bring your best self to every situation, and to find strength in vulnerability.

This isn't just a book about Maggie's career shift—it's a story about life, about embracing change, and about finding meaning in the work we do. Knowing Maggie as I do, I can tell you this book is a true reflection of who she is: strong, compassionate, and deeply committed to making a difference. I'm so excited for you to read her story, and I know you'll come away just as inspired as I have been by her journey.

Laurel Hurd
President & CEO of Interface and Board Member at THOR Industries

Humbled
— on —
Purpose

CHAPTER 1

FIGHTING FOR A (MASSIVE) PAY CUT

HUMBLING. People like to have a word for the new year or even a motivating phrase for the month or year. I will often change my computer password to some positive mantra so that I must start each day typing an upbeat message to myself. None of that would have made a difference in the spring of 2016. Humbling came barreling toward me and knocked me over as if I were a bowling pin. Nearly everything about that summer screamed *humbling*.

In May of that year, I walked out of the work home I'd loved for fourteen years, with all of my personal belongings in a single copy paper box. One of my former team members, Molly Kesmodel, lived by the single-box rule, which was to never have more items in your office than you can remove in a single copy-paper box because who wants to return to clean out your office after being canned. Plus there is always an empty copy-paper box around. Her philosophy was you just never know when you might "get quit."

GETTING "QUIT"

"Getting quit" is my WBF (*work best friend* and regular bestie too) and former co-worker Jo Ann Herold's colloquialism for being terminated, and we all used it because it sounds nicer than getting fired, terminated or even laid off. Unlike Molly's single-box theory, which helps in case of a surprise dismissal, I knew that I was going to "get quit" because the writing was on the wall.

I was working for my fourth CEO in two years. Changing bosses is the equivalent of changing companies. And this latest *company* (i.e. boss), did not care for me. I had gradually brought the big stuff home, leaving only a few family pictures in my beautiful office in the building where I had led both the real-estate search and renovation project just a couple years earlier.

FIGHTING FOR A (MASSIVE) PAY CUT

Some might wonder why I cleared out my office and waited rather than just quitting, which is a fair question. After fourteen years with a company pouring your blood, sweat, tears and heart into its success, maybe a small part of me held out hope that things might turn around. Maybe I was expecting the new boss to see what others had seen in me. Surely the new boss would soon see me as the heart and soul of the place. Nope, it didn't happen. Plus, there are these severance agreements that nobody talks about and everyone hopes for—and are worth waiting on.

So I hung around with my great title, beautiful albeit now minimalist, office, highly respected company, and an amazing team of people that I loved, while my self-esteem shrunk and the new CEO got ready to tell me to pack my copy box. When the day finally came, I was called into the CEO's office. They had previously canceled all regularly scheduled weekly meetings because they did not believe in meeting "just to meet." They said they would tell me when they wanted to meet, which to that point over the past three months had been almost never.

But today, before a 2 p.m. leadership team meeting, they wanted to meet with just me. Hmmm. I went to lunch and told a friend that I was pretty sure I was getting fired that day. When I returned to my desk, I had an email from Delta

Air Lines that my tickets to an upcoming company conference the following month had been canceled. That was another pretty glaring sign. Glad they got that handled before they let me know officially. I'd hate for them to pay a late fee by waiting until I actually walked out the door.

So I was called in and when I came out, I didn't work for one of America's most beloved brands any longer. I can't say much more about it than that because of severance agreements and such, but it was neither pleasant nor hostile. I don't think that I cried at all, not even once I got into the car. I was mostly just relieved that the big wait was over. While waiting for the other shoe to drop might be worth it financially, I don't recommend it as a mental-health-building activity.

In fact, I strongly recommend leaving places that make you unhappy before they make you anxious, miserable, and doubt yourself. I stayed too long. Yet even as I left this place that had been the pinnacle of my corporate career; where most of my team knew my Starbucks order (Venti breve misto with sugar-free cinnamon dolce), I knew that I did not want to re-create this same level of privileged work.

Even as my executive assistant held back tears as I carried my single box out the door, I wanted my life to point away from one with an executive assistant who shielded me from time vultures, made my travel arrangements, knew my food preferences, and spoke with my children's nanny regularly. As I pulled out of my unofficial parking spot (we did not have assigned parking spots, yet nobody ever parked in that first spot on the left side of the building because they knew that is where I usually parked) I was acutely aware of the fact that I was *not* going to work anywhere that had assigned parking, executive assistants, or lots of perks. I was as excited about that as one can be while being asked to leave the building.

Most of all, it was not about what I would be giving up in a new role, but what I wanted to take on. Is it too much to say that I wanted to make a difference in the world? At the very least, I wanted to make a difference in my world, in my community, of this I was certain.

Plus, I was armed with twenty-five years of human resources experience, fifteen years of operational leadership experience, including ten years of C-suite skills. I also had immense volunteer leadership experience, so even though I was aware of the bias against nonprofits hiring from the corporate world, I was confident there were nonprofit agencies out there that would find my skills not just transferable, but valuable. If I am 100 percent honest, I confess that I thought any nonprofit would be lucky to have me. Or, if not me, then certainly my experience and skills.

THE DIFFERENCES BETWEEN THE NONPROFIT AND CORPORATE WORLDS

It didn't take long after leaving one of America's most beloved brands, (HoneyBaked for those of you that didn't read the book description), to experience one of the first great barriers to serving in the nonprofit world; the total devaluation of experience from the corporate world. It actually goes both ways and it is hardwired.

Candidates from the corporate world come bearing highly transferable skills but often lack the required humility that it takes to make their case that they are really ready to jump into the nonprofit sector. Meanwhile, hiring managers, boards and recruiters in the nonprofit industry have a strong belief that unless you have grown up in the not-for-profit industry, or have some arbitrarily assigned, requisite number of years of experience in it, you are not even worthy of an interview.

This is where I found myself in July 2016 as I interviewed for the Executive Director's role with the Child Development Association (which we would eventually rebrand to become the Children's Development Academy).

FIGHTING FOR A (MASSIVE) PAY CUT

My career coach, Dutch Earle, had told me about the opening and suggested that this might be the passion role for which I was looking. Even though I thought that I wanted to be connected with causes related to women in leadership, mental health, or food insecurity, early education became appealing to me as I learned more about it. I was very intrigued at the impact high-quality early education plays in the community as a root-cause solution to many long-term issues. When asked, I told my friend Dutch to please forward my resume. My enthusiasm was returned with a kind rejection.

The humbling continued.

In hindsight, I did not lack humility when it came to approaching this job, nor any nonprofit opportunity. I was raised in retail. I can work in a stockroom with boxes imported from Miami that include roaches bigger than my thumb. I can unclog a toilet in the restroom and get a kid's shoelace or small Croc out of an escalator pretty darn quick when called upon. My first career role out of college was at the Macy's store in the Lenox Square Mall in Atlanta where my department included boys, toddlers and the yogurt stand which was next to the escalators. Trust me when I say that I am not above cleaning up a mess. Even as the president of HoneyBaked, I would often pick up litter in the parking lot on my way to visit a store. My nature is to be hands on and roll up my sleeves.

Also, in preparation for my desired industry change, I had interviewed friends who had successfully made the transition from corporate to nonprofit to learn about how they had succeeded and what to avoid along the way. I studied successes like Amy Dosik at the Girl Scouts and Virginia Hepner at the Woodruff Arts Center, both executives who had made very successful transitions. They talked about the pitfalls, the importance of having a supportive board, and the pace of change being much slower in the not-for-profit sector. By and large, though, they were very happy with their decisions and flourishing.

So I was very surprised when the CDA search team didn't even want to speak with me. I'm not suggesting that being the President and Chief Operating Officer of one of America's most beloved brands, which generated over half a billion dollars in revenue, qualified me by itself to run the $2 million nonprofit that funded an early education center. However, I had also started a highly successful foundation at our local elementary school, served as president of a local junior service league and served on the local school governance council. I had already demonstrated a passion for education. In fact, not to toot my own horn, but I had been awarded the state of Georgia PTA's highest honor, The Visionary Leadership Award, based on leading advocacy activities around redistricting. I didn't just wake up one morning in 2016 and decide to get involved in my community—I had done it my entire life. As someone who'd done a lot of hiring in her life, I was surprised.

Luckily, our mutual friend was even more surprised and annoyed than I was. He reached out to the hiring team and suggested that perhaps as a local educational advocate, they might introduce me to their organization and invite me for a tour, which they promptly did; I happily accepted. Somewhere a couple classrooms into the tour, it became a walking interview and at the end, the board chair asked if they could reconsider their rejection and send me to interview with their recruiter, which I enthusiastically obliged.

A few days later, driving down to the recruiter's office, I thought about the conversations that I had with my husband Bob about my next career stop that morning. I was focused on finding a role that did work that "mattered," which I defined as likely being in the nonprofit sector or perhaps with the foundation arm of a for-profit corporation. The job needed to use my leadership skills to help people who were on the margins of society.

For a long time, one Bible verse had been my North

Star. "To whom much is given, much will be required," from Luke 12:48. When others tried to thank me for any "generosity," I would cite this verse, because the truth is that it is easy to write a check when you are making a lot of money. I felt a deep push from the clock and from God that it was time to put my boots on the ground and do more than give generously. I also knew intimately that life is short. My boys were quickly growing up and out. I wanted to plant my work closer to home now, while they were still around, to enjoy time with them.

For years I had found ways to make my work at HoneyBaked, Circuit City, Belk, and Macy's be about the people that worked there and the customers and communities that we served. However, I was now looking to do more. I had set three absolutes with Bob. First, I did not want extensive travel. My sons were in high school and playing competitive baseball. I had sacrificed a lot already and I wanted to be home more. Secondly, we live in the northern Atlanta suburbs and was looking for something that was not ITP (inside the perimeter). I was determined to avoid a nasty commute where I would waste hours of my day traveling. Even if I used the time to listen to great books or better myself, a long commute was a deal breaker. Lastly, I wanted to do work that mattered and that made a difference in my community more than selling pork, electronics or widgets.

I wanted to work in an organization possessing a great culture, or at a place where I could create one, where people loved to come to work each day and cared about the work and their co-workers. I would not work at an organization that was solely motivated by profit, did not care about people, and did not think long term about mission and the community. Most of all, I wanted to do work that made a difference in people's lives who'd been marginalized, preferably in my own community.

A SEMINAL (YET UNCONVENTIONAL) INTERVIEW QUESTION

When I arrived in the recruiter's office (we'll call him Mike), I was surprised by his welcome. He greeted me warmly and then quickly changed gears. He said that, "We both know you can do the CDA job with your eyes closed. What I want to talk to you about is an exciting seven-figure job that you would be perfect for and their CEO would hire you today." Mike went on to explain that he had spoken to the CEO and he was very excited about the prospect of an experienced HR executive who had also had experience owning the P&L.

He went on to describe a job opening for a Chief Human Resource Officer at a very well known local retailer. The position was located in midtown Atlanta, an hour-long commute from my home each way without rain or an accident. Strike one. The company had locations all over the U.S. and Canada, so heavy travel would likely be required. Strike two. Worst of all, when he identified the company, I recognized it as one known for a fairly brutal, commission-driven culture with a top-down leadership model. Strike three.

I didn't bat an eye. I don't know if I was so affected by a few months of time off, or so steadfast in what I wanted to do next, but the million-dollar annual package did not sway my thinking at all. I did not consider for a moment interviewing for the role. I was probably so shocked that the recruiter had tried to poach a candidate that I barely thought about the lucrative opportunity.

Without even discussing it with my husband, I quietly but decisively turned down the job that would be an increase over my last job and told him that I wanted to pursue the nonprofit role at the CDA, which was an 86 percent pay cut compared to my previous role. For those of you checking my math, I made well into the high six figures in 2015 and was now chasing a job advertising a top rate of $100,000.

Nonprofits have to list executive salaries on their 990 forms, so there is no hiding my current compensation, although the 990 includes benefits and such. Mike was very surprised and said "Well, you passed the test," inferring that he had only been testing my resolve to go into the nonprofit industry. However, I know for a fact that the job he described was open, and he was recruiting for it. While he might have been walking an ethical tightrope, he also helped me clarify my priorities.

When I returned home that evening and told Bob what had happened, he gently asked if I was sure that I didn't have another couple years of a "big job" in me. While I wasn't sure that I didn't, I also knew that I didn't want to do that right now. I had a calling to do something different. While nonprofit leadership certainly isn't a sabbatical, I felt like I was being called for a mission-type of an assignment in the corporate world. It might sound pompous to call myself a corporate missionary when I would still be earning six figures, but giving up millions of dollars in annual earning potential in your prime earning years isn't nothing. I'm proud of the work that my entire family has done, and the sacrifices that we've made together.

My summer of humbling does end happily, even humorously. The advertised pay range was $86,000 to $100,000 as Executive Director. Several days later, after another couple rounds of panel interviews, Mike called and offered me the CDA's Executive Director role at $86,000. I remember chuckling when I responded, "My husband can only take so much."

I told him that I'd be thrilled to accept the Executive Director role at $100,000 and I would like them to add the CEO title to the role as well. Most nonprofit executives were now operating more in that capacity and that title was an important asset for external communication. The board quickly agreed. I started in November and began a long first year that was more challenging than I thought, but I learned more than I could have ever imagined.

THE TRUTH ABOUT THE PERCEIVED DIFFERENCES BETWEEN NONPROFITS AND FOR-PROFIT COMPANIES

It became clear to me during the interview process, and during my time serving in both industries, that there is nothing uniquely special about nonprofit agencies or for-profit companies. For-profit companies could be starkly different from one another and actually more similar to a nonprofit. For example, I think that leaving the CDA and going to work for Chick-fil-A would be easier than leaving Chick-fil-A to work for some other for-profit companies. This is because Chick-fil-A is so purpose-driven and has such a people-focused culture. How a company divides shareholder dividends is not the greatest common denominator for determining candidate fit.

I encourage hiring managers for nonprofits and for-profits to drop the preconceived notions that someone's industry experience limits their future ability to assimilate into any organization or industry. Each individual is as different as each company. Assess them accordingly. Good candidates are too hard to find—don't eliminate an entire class based upon industry affiliation.

I would also consider what a good for-profit candidate brings in terms of their contacts and connections. My network has been invaluable to the CDA and has more than made up for any ramp-up time in learning the nuances of the nonprofit sector. Do not underestimate this gift. I was able to dial for donations from day one.

CHAPTER 2

LIFE IS SHORT
(MINE WAS UNFAIR EARLY)

I WAS fifty-three when I left my favorite job. I was too young and motivated to fully retire but acutely aware of how short life is. I had already exceeded my birth mother's longevity by twenty-two years and my father's life span by five years, so I was definitely living on house money in my own mind. I felt each day was a gift of time, especially in a recently unhappy work situation.

Some might feel like they have the luxury of working a few more years and then doing "good works" once they retire or start their chapters of "significance" later. I knew that I may never get to see the playing years of my kids' high school baseball careers or summers at the lake. In fact, I woke up most days feeling that I might die tomorrow, so I needed to make the most of today. This meant being around to see my boys run out in the Roswell High School Hornets baseball starting lineup, go to prom, and drive them to school before they got their driver's licenses. This is where some of our best conversations occurred, in the morning car rides.

Why did I wake up so acutely aware that each day could be my last? Well, I was practically born into that situation in the Midwest. I mean the real Midwest. Burlington, Iowa to be exact. It is a small city located in the southeastern corner of Iowa on the banks of the Mississippi River. Every summer it hosts Steamboat Days. Its claim to fame is Snake Alley that replicates another famous Snake Alley in San Francisco. Or maybe San Francisco copied Burlington? Who's to say?

My family was English, Irish and German immigrants just a generation off the farm. My dad was a pretty strict disciplinarian who had a favorite quote that "lying was worse than murder in his eyes." I swear. Sometimes, if someone wouldn't admit to who left the blinds open in the bathroom or who ate the last chocolate chip cookie, my siblings and I would be lined up to play "Truth or Consequences (ToC)" which involved a belt and beatings until someone confessed. Sometimes I would confess to things that I did not do to shorten the number of rounds of ToC. Just setting the scene here.

FAMILY DYNAMICS

My birth mom, Mary, died when I was ten months old. My brother, Dan, was five years old and my sister Nancy, was six years old. My dad, left to raise three children on his own, remarried when I was three years old. He brought our new mom (Carol) home, introduced her as our mom and directed us all to call her mom. That was that. This was the 1960s. There was no family counseling, long transition or deep discussions about our feelings.

Previously, Dad had employed a nanny to take care of us while he worked. If you are imagining Mary Poppins, think again. Dorothy Brown was very large, poorly educated, highly affordable to my single working father, and uniquely qualified to give the three of us what we needed most: unconditional love when we desperately needed it. Monopoly games lasted forever with Dorothy because she did not understand the decimals and everyone got $2,000 for passing GO. But we all loved her, and she loved us back. When I think back on her big face, I think of a cherub angel watching over us.

When Carol came, Dorothy left with only a short transition during which time there was a bit of a power play between who was in charge. Carol would put my hair in pigtails and Dorothy would restyle it into a ponytail. My dad couldn't take too much of this, so the transition did not last as long as was planned. It was another deep loss for me when Dorothy was suddenly gone, although Carol did her best to fill the void.

Many years later I tried to track Dorothy down with the help of my Aunt Sue. We found that she had been buried without a stone in a pauper's grave in the same cemetery as my Grandpa Smith in Burlington, Iowa. It was a privilege to be able to purchase a stone for her that said she was loved by Nancy, Danny and Margaret because she was and is.

After Carol moved in, we were to call her mom from then on and never talk about our "other" mom, not that we were allowed to speak of her much previously. When my little brother Ben was born a year later, we were then a family of six and there was no mention of half-siblings, step siblings or anything other than brothers and sisters. That is still how I feel about my family today.

In fact, I have even added a bonus sister. In 2020, I learned through Ancestry.com that we had an older sister in Arizona, named Deb who was born of a high school relationship between her mom and our dad. I was privileged to meet her in the fall of 2023, and she has since joined our dysfunctional family text chains and camaraderie. Deb is my sister, although we missed out on being raised together. Likewise, my little brother Ben (who also goes by Chris) and I are closer in some ways than my full blooded older siblings. We are a big dysfunctional family, and I would not have it any other way.

Carol, my *new* mom, although truly the only mom that I have ever known and loved, had amazing parents who immediately took to their new roles as our grandma and grandpa. I remember them both with so much love. I was their "little Dutch dolly," and they gave me a safe harbor during a very tumultuous time of much change in my life.

Rarely, I would gain the courage to timidly ask Carol, Grandma, or Grandpa about my "birth" mom—usually when my dad was safely out of earshot. I learned that she was a teacher and that she had beautiful auburn hair, but not much more. Sometimes, I would hear the adults talking about Mary and catch words like colicky baby, accidental pregnancy, and nervous breakdown. Sometimes, when I would get more specific to ask how she died, I was told it was a car accident, a heart attack, or a fall down the stairs, depending upon who I asked. None of this lessened my curiosity.

I remember asking my slightly older next-door neighbor and my self-declared, best friend, Molly, if she knew what happened to my birth mom. She told me with much superiority that she was not allowed to talk to me about it. However, Molly, whose family was devoutly Roman Catholic, was apparently allowed to tell me that Mary was burning in Hell. She was also free to mention that since I had not yet been baptized, if I died, I was going to Limbo with the other unbaptized babies. This was not reassuring to an eight-year-old as I imagined myself floating somewhere in a giant snow globe surrounded by infants. You can imagine why I urged my parents to get me baptized at fourteen.

For those wondering why I didn't just ask my dad, I haven't yet painted the entire picture beyond Truth or Consequences. My dad was involved in a horrible car accident while my mom Mary, who was pregnant with me, already had two small children to care for and was in the middle of moving homes. Dad was lucky to be alive but with a newly paralyzed right arm, he blamed himself for the pressure that Mary experienced while he recuperated in the V.A. hospital. After Mary passed, he didn't always handle his guilt and anger well, which is an understatement on par with describing the pope as merely Catholic.

To be clear, my dad was a highly functional alcoholic who most days was a great and loving father and a good man but could be triggered (or maybe without trigger) to also become a pretty mean drunk. When triggered, he often would take it out on his family. Obviously we tip-toed around things that would trigger him, like talk of Mary. We also escaped into the closets late at night when he would come home from the bar until we could assess his mood. It seems very tragic to write this, but it was just our normal existence at the time. It didn't happen every night or even every week. My mom Carol took the brunt of it, but I've been beaten for no reason in the middle of the night more than I care to recall, both after being found hiding in the closet and sometimes when I failed to awaken in time to hide. That saying about what doesn't kill you makes you stronger, well I was one strong cookie by the time I was five years old.

Dad was always very sorry the next day as we pretended that nothing happened. You get the idea now why I might not have approached him about something that might have gotten me whacked or even the belt for even asking the question. Plus it had zero probability of gaining an answer.

But eventually, I did get an answer.

FINDING OUT THE TRUTH

I remember the day and the time so clearly when the truth literally landed in my lap. I was in my early teens, after we had moved north up the Mississippi River to LaCrosse, Wisconsin, for my dad's career with Trane Company. We were living a comfortable life on the foot of the bluffs with a swimming pool and experiencing fewer angry episodes from my dad. I was in junior high school. I was a cheerleader with a hockey player boyfriend and, as the T-shirt says, "Life was Good." I was still aware that my family was blended and every now and then I would be mad at my adopted mom, as teenage girls often are at their moms, blood-related or not. I would occasionally pine for my red-haired birth mom who was a teacher and who I thought would surely have understood me better, but that was all about to end.

It was the summer, and I was sitting on the floor in our basement looking for a book to read. Carol instilled a huge love of reading in me and we would often visit the library together. But this day I was in the basement looking for a book when I saw a white leather book on the bookcase that attracted my attention so I pulled it out. As I pulled out the

LIFE IS SHORT (MINE WAS UNFAIR EARLY)

book and opened it, the first thing that I noticed was the tissue paper between each page and the silk lining with beautiful writing. I saw my birth mom's name—Mary Francis Wasson Michaels—written on the front inside cover in gorgeous calligraphy followed by her date of birth and the date of her death, November 25, 1963. Historians might immediately recognize that this was the date of John F. Kennedy's funeral. Thirteen-year old Maggie Michaels did not recognize this and kept flipping the pages. As I flipped the pages, a yellowed piece of paper from a newspaper fluttered to the floor beside me onto the basement carpeting.

I picked it up and began to read the words from the paper and suddenly all the half-truths and full-on lies made sense to my adolescent brain. I was reading my mother's obituary that had fallen out of her funeral book. The obituary was not written in the kindly vernacular of modern-day journalism. It did not say that Mary Michaels died suddenly, nor did it leave the cause of death mercifully silent. It stated that Mary Francis Wasson Michaels of 809 North Sixth Street, Burlington, Iowa was found hanging from a gas pipe in the basement of her home at 809 North 6th Street, leaving behind her husband and three children; Nancy, 6; Daniel, 5; and Margaret, 1.

This was a lie. Not that Mary had hung herself that day.

That was true. But I was not yet one year old. I could not walk, talk, or feed myself. I was a ten-month-old baby, technically an infant. I was not even a toddler yet when I was voluntarily abandoned and left alone in the world by the person who was supposed to love me more than life itself. Agape, unconditional love is what mothers are supposed to feel for their babies, but not my mother. At least not toward me anyway. This was how I felt that summer day in our basement.

I don't remember crying. I do remember feeling incredible anger and betrayal. I also remember an unexpected taste in my mouth that was foul and bitter. I put the book back quickly as I knew that it was forbidden, but I could not unknow what I had just learned. Right then, as a thirteen-year-old, I had a new truth which made it difficult to breathe.

All the times that people would not tell me how my mother died, they were protecting me from this truth. The words unplanned pregnancy, colicky baby and nervous breakdown had new meaning to me. Even the monogram on my robe, triple "M" for Margaret Marie Michaels—which my dad *joked* stood for Mistake, Mistake, Mistake—was now a knife through my heart. I probably was a mistake. As irrational as it seems, I felt responsible for my mother's death. Hard stop. This feeling that is impossible to understand did not go away for a very long time.

Intellectually I knew then, and I know now, that a ten-month old baby cannot kill anyone, let alone her own mother. But I also felt with conviction that she would still be alive if I had never been born. Maybe the stress would not have triggered suicide. Certainly there would have been no postpartum depression or psychosis, which I learned later was what she had suffered from. I also realized that her stress was probably exacerbated by my colic. Certainly, no colicky baby and no postpartum mental illness could have meant no suicide. Even now, I do not feel differently about this set of facts, but I no longer hold myself responsible.

PROVING MYSELF

This began a multi-decade journey to deserve my place on this planet and even the air that I breathed. This is not hyperbole. I felt an immediate sense of needing to make my life count and count big. I owed it to my dad, my brother, and my sister to make up for their loss. Ironically, I did not feel like I owed anything to Mary. I did not understand mental illness enough to feel anything but anger towards her. How could she leave Nancy and Danny, even if it was all my fault? What kind of a mother does that? It would be many years, several therapists and a spiritual awakening before I came to really understand what happened with my mother and accept that it was neither her fault nor mine.

In the meantime, I set out on a mission of perfectionism and accomplishment; attempting to control as many things as possible as I could, like earning straight A's, dating the star athlete and Homecoming king, becoming a class office holder, sorority president, panhellenic president, etc. At every step and milestone, I attempted to justify my existence through achievement and control.

Another move for our family was precipitated by my dad becoming the president of a privately owned boiler manufacturer. This did not make my quest to be all things to all people easy. We moved in the middle of eighth grade from a school where I was already a cheerleader with a tight circle of friends, headed for show choir, a top student and queen of the hill and forced to a new state and new school with a new social order, Spring Lake Junior High in western Michigan. I was starting over.

I still remember my first day vividly. I walked into the social studies classroom, unaware that my previous school's dress code of skirts, sweaters, stockings and handbags for girls was not the norm in this new school. Instead I was met by a room full of students in jeans, Lands' End sweaters, and sneakers. One cute but obnoxious boy with olive skin, dark hair and bright blue eyes asked me if I was a student teacher. I simply glared at him as I found a seat in the back of the class. I barely survived the day, missing my friends and my hockey playing, braces wearing boyfriend that I had sworn to love forever well before the days of texting, social media and Snapchat.

As I got ready to go meet my mom for pick up that afternoon, I went to the wrong side of the school and had to walk by the same obnoxious boy with the bright blue eyes and dark hair, surrounded by his posse as I made my way to the correct pick up location. He called out to me with a very personal "Hey, new girl!" I turned my head to look as I kept walking. "What's so important inside that purse that you have to carry it around all day?" he asked. Without a second thought, he received the entirety of my frustration for the past eight hours as I glibly responded, "tampons!" and continued walking toward the exit. His friends punched him and laughingly said, "she got you!" I did not turn back but might have slightly smiled to myself for the first time that day.

That night my dad asked if I made any friends to which I replied, "definitely no." He then asked if there were any cute boys. I told him that there was one cute boy that I talked to that day but he was a total jerk. The next day, the jerk was much nicer to me and we eventually became friends. He told me about his 18-foot long jump and I told him about my brother Dan's 22-foot-10-inch long jump. This process of him trying to impress me, and me trying to humble him, continued for the remainder of the school year.

I am now married to that jerk and have been for thirty-eight years, ironically. We started dating in tenth grade because, as one of my male neighbor friends advised me, you were the last cute girl to move in and he had already dated everyone else in our small town. Not exactly the best reason to be chosen, but we are opposites who attract and it works.

While I was never a cheerleader at my new school or on top of the popularity food chain, I had a couple of beloved friends who are still friends today. I was an officer of the National Honor Society, ironically giving a speech during my senior year on the importance of service. I was also voted most likely to succeed in large part due to my drive, grades, and SAT scores. Meanwhile, I dated (and eventually married) the best athlete in our school, who was the Homecoming king with the best smile and prettiest eyes.

Through high school, things were going pretty well. I felt that the more I could control the world the more I would prevent bad things from happening to me, but life wasn't done testing me just yet. The next terrible and truly horrible thing happened before my senior year of high school was over. It was a whopper. Nothing can top my first bad year of life, but this was a very nasty second place.

A TRULY AWFUL SENIOR YEAR CHRISTMAS

I was half way through my senior year in high school when the universe decided to see how much more I could handle. Bob had been named a first team all-state running back thanks in part to my dad calling in his stats from our small western Michigan town every Monday morning to the Detroit newspapers, like he had done with my older brother in Wisconsin. Now Bob was exploring college football and baseball offers. I had tested well and my dad was determined that my SAT scores were the ticket to a place at a school like MIT or another highly rated engineering school. I told him that I wanted to be an attorney and he told me that I should get an engineering degree and then be an environmental attorney. It seemed like as good a plan as any. I had long ago learned that arguing with my dad was a bad idea, so MIT didn't seem like such a bad option, relatively.

Before we knew it, it was Christmas Eve which was a big deal at our house. We usually started opening presents a couple weeks beforehand. We started with the gifts from out-of-town relatives that would send socks or other lame items, in a kid's eye, and worked our way up to items that were more fun. (I'm glad I waited until my Aunt Pat passed to write my book. We always opened her gifts first.)

On December 24, 1980, at 3 a.m. technically now on Christmas Eve morning, my dad and mom came home, happily tipsy, having been out celebrating my mom's December 23rd birthday. Dad roused my little brother, Ben, and I from bed to open our biggest Christmas gifts early. I had recently taken an interest in photography and my "big" gift was a Canon AE1 SLR camera which I opened in the early morning hours of Christmas Eve while my dad looked on happily. My brother opened a remote-control airplane while my parents smiled and watched. I had my dad open his gift, a framed still shot of our husky mix dog, Bar, catching a ball in mid air that I had taken and developed myself. He admired my work and was genuinely pleased. We shared a special love of our dogs.

My dad loved Christmas and opening gifts. He loved seeing his children enjoy a different life than he had growing up on a small farm in Iowa as the youngest of two boys. His older brother was afforded a college education while my dad went into the military. He then returned and started, literally, in the mail room at Murray Iron Works and worked his way up to become the President of Johnston Boiler Company. He was a self-made man and he was determined that his kids would have a different path. When he wasn't the occasional angry, violent alcoholic, he was an amazing, generous, and loving father who adored his family, friends and his dogs. In the early morning hours of December 24th, 1980, he was this loving, generous father and I am so blessed to have these as final memories.

Ben and I thanked our parents, kissed them goodnight and told them both that we loved them and they told us that they loved us. We went back to bed about 4:30 am. Hours later, when we awoke for the real Christmas Eve, my older sister Nancy and older brother Dan returned home to celebrate Christmas and we waited for my dad to join us and open the rest of our gifts.

Even as it got dark, my dad didn't rouse to unwrap gifts which was unusual. My mom went into their room to wake him and immediately called my older brother Dan for help. She then agitatedly told us to stay in the living room as she called 911. I remember the ambulance screaming up the snow-covered driveway and the EMTs racing in with the stretcher. I also remember them leaving with the empty stretcher and the sirens silent as a hearse and a medical examiner pulled in to take their place.

I called my boyfriend of two years, Bob, to tell him what had happened, but his family had a very standard-issue

Midwestern police scanner, thus he already knew. He was on his way across the snow-covered railroad tracks before I hung up the phone.

I was seventeen years old when I became a biological orphan, due to my dad's widowmaker heart attack. The fact that it was on Christmas Eve just added an extra insult to the event and has prevented me from ever successfully singing Silent Night with a candle in church without sobbing, although the birth of my own children lessened the sobbing to just tears running down my face.

When his obituary ran, it listed that he was preceded in death by his first wife Mary. This was the first time many of my friends learned that Carol was my adopted mother. This was fine with me as I still had no use for Mary. My dad's death only upped my desire for control to whatever the score is for "off the charts." My need to earn my place on earth was now combined with an obsession to to prevent bad things from entering my life again.

The desire to control all things apparently is the birth of great leadership skills and an incredible foundation to a career in business leadership. It is not an especially attractive component for little girls, although I am so thrilled to see the current campaigns to stop trying to keep little girls from being "bossy." These characteristics can also be challenging for one's overall mental health and happiness which I struggled with for years to come.

CHAPTER 3

HAIL TO THE VICTORS, LEADERS AND BEST (YEARS)

SHORTLY after my dad's death, I followed Bob to Hope College in Holland, Michigan, where he played football. It was a good academic school close to home because I thought my mom might need me that first year. It turns out that she did not. Meanwhile, I didn't do much research on Hope College.

I was surprised when we had orientation in the chapel. Only later did I learn that Hope is affiliated with the Reformed Church in America, a branch of the Dutch Reformed Church, a fairly conservative Christian denomination. At the time, even before Chick-Fil-A being closed on Sundays was normal to me, Holland, Michigan was a ghost town on Sunday. These folks took not working on Sundays more seriously than most.

A FRESHMAN YEAR WITHOUT MUCH HOPE OR HAPPINESS

While Hope's website says that students of all faiths and no faith are welcome there, I did not experience that, nor did Bob. Hope didn't allow men in the girls' dorms, had strict rules surrounding alcohol anywhere on campus and near mandatory membership in some Christian organizations to participate in campus athletics and Greek life. I found these and a myriad of other rules stifling—and I was not exactly a party animal.

That difficult first year after my dad's death, which now included enrollment at a very strange school, was capped off by being a no-bid for the local sorority that I really wanted to join in a final attempt to try to fit in at this odd institution. I still remember learning their songs and really wanting to join their little house.

When I finished crying, I called my mom and told her I was taking a year off college with a plan to take a gap year, working on Mackinac Island. My mom had been enjoying a bit of a second childhood after my dad's death, experiencing a newfound freedom herself, so I was fully expecting a response along the lines of "That's fine, Maggie, honey." I was floored when she said I had to return to Hope or find somewhere else to go that fall, but I was definitely *not* dropping out, even for a year. Well, I was *not* going back to Hope. However, I also knew this was something that I could control one way or another.

So, after committing the ultimate act of personal defiance in 1982, getting my ears double pierced, I got in my Buick Regal and drove three hours to Ann Arbor where I sat in the admissions office and waited for someone to talk to me, without an appointment. I told them my sad story about being an orphan and begged them to let me in. After grabbing a tissue for themselves and me, they politely offered to review my application.

They then kindly handed me a clipboard, a pen and waited while I completed it. Then they whisked me in for an interview. Before I left the admissions office, I had a commitment that if my second-semester grades were as good as my first, I could start that fall in Ann Arbor. I was thrilled and relieved.

I look back now and wonder, *Who was that brave nineteen-year-old girl? Where did she get the gumption to do that, the hutz-*

pah? The truth is that I didn't look at any of these things as brave, but rather necessary to do what needed to be done for the next step in my life. I had been in survival mode since I was a baby. I needed to get the heck out of Holland, Michigan, to survive, in my mind. So that's what I did.

A FRESH START IN MAIZE AND BLUE

Looking back, some of my happiest years began that fall when I enrolled at the University of Michigan. I rushed again and I was determined that I was going to experience sorority life come Hell or highwater as we say along the banks of the Mississippi River.

One of my funniest experiences during rush at Michigan happened with a girl that became my friend because we were alphabetically paired by last name (whom I'll call Polly). Polly and I entered the Sigma Delta Tau (SDT) house together. I was escorted away, handed a bowl of M&Ms and sat in the corner, largely left to my own devices. Polly, a pretty brunette from the Detroit suburbs, was escorted around the room and introduced to lots of sisters. I could only stare at these beautiful sorority girls while popping M&Ms, having never seen quite so many beautiful dark haired girls before in one place. Certainly not in Iowa, Wisconsin, the westside of Michigan, and definitely not at Hope College.

HAIL TO THE VICTORS—LEADERS AND BEST (YEARS)

As we left the house, I mentioned to Polly that those girls were "gorgeous," to which she simply nodded. I then remarked that nobody spoke to me. She then said nonchalantly, "You might try losing the cross before we go to the AEPi house, blondie." When I asked her what she meant, she informed me that the SDT house was an all-Jewish sorority in Ann Arbor (that is not the case everywhere), and my blonde hair and cross necklace was the equivalent of a "no trespassing" sign for them. I was shocked. I had no idea there was such a thing as an all-Jewish sorority.

My best friend in elementary school in Lacrosse, Wisconsin had been Jewish, which just meant eating better tasting, all-beef kosher hotdogs at Girl Scout events with her, a sacrifice which I was happy to make in the spirit of integration. My brother's best friend in Lacrosse was also Jewish. But we certainly didn't have enough Jewish friends, to my knowledge, to have an entire club. Catholics, Lutherans and Friday night fish frys during Lent ruled Western Wisconsin. It was quite eye-opening to me to learn that there were entire sorority chapters based upon religion. Later, in my own sorority, one of my little sisters in the sorority was Jewish and one third of our chapter of Chi Omega was Jewish, about the same as the University of Michigan.

So after I opened my eyes to the fact that I was not likely to get a bid to SDT or AEPi, I was wide open to the other sixteen sororities. I was shocked when, after nearly two years of nothing but bad news and unhappiness, I got my first choice, Chi Omega. It's hard to explain the unmitigated joy that I felt when I opened that bid envelope; the feeling of belonging that I had been seeking for a very long time. My pledge sisters are still some of my dearest friends and my days spent at 1525 Washtenaw Avenue are among those I count as some of the happiest of my life. I found another family, finally.

A RUSH OF PERSONAL GROWTH

I know that isn't the case for everyone. For some young women rush is a hideous experience. My first rush was hideous, but I own some of that in hindsight. I only wanted one sorority and was not open to the possibilities of other chapters being a better fit for me because I was so intent on being in a certain chapter. I rejected four other sororities and 'suicided' one, meaning only put that one chapter on my final bid card. That is almost always a bad decision.

Chi Omega was not the top sorority on campus when I joined, but it felt right to me and I might say that it was at the top when our pledge class graduated. Our pledge class and the classes before it and those after us created something special. You have to decide to build something. If you drop out because you don't get into the top house, you are losing out on not just four years of amazing opportunities to build something, you are missing out on a lifetime of incredible memories. I believe this with all of my pro-Greek heart.

I say this because in Ann Arbor, I moved into my beautiful sorority house and was immediately slated to become president of the Chi Omega chapter. My sorority sisters saw leadership in me that I didn't even know existed. I was so confident in *their* assessment that I subsequently ran for President of the Panhellenic Association the following year and won because of their support and campaigning. The value of a small group of supportive sisters living together and cheering you on at a large university cannot be overstated. Two of the best decisions of my life were made in the fall of 1982, transferring to the University of Michigan and pledging Chi Omega.

After being elected president of Chi Omega and president of the women's Greek system, I was also selected for a number of other elite honors like Adara, the tower society, based on leadership and achievement. I'm also very proud that during my Panhellenic leadership, we invited another sorority, Sigma Kappa, to expand on campus and re-colonized Alpha Xi Delta, allowing 200 more women to experience sorority life.

When I stood in front of the women at the Michigan Union that came to learn about a "new" sorority on campus and announced that we were re-colonizing Alpha Xi Delta, there was palpable disappointment as they had a pre-existing negative reputation on campus. However, when I told them that their *new* Alpha Xi pledge class would be "carried in"—the traditional way new members are welcomed to their new home—by one of the best fraternities on campus, Sigma Nu, there was a unified squeal of acknowledgement. This was, indeed, a new day for Alpha Xi Delta.

How did I get the Sigma Nu's to commit to that?

A few weeks after pledging Chi Omega, I called Bob, who was still at Hope in Holland, to advise him that I was going to a hayride with a Sigma Epsilon (Sig Ep) that Friday night. He asked if the Chi Omega's are going with the Sig Eps, I said no, just a few of us with a few of them. He quickly understood that I was going on a date to which he strongly objected and immediately began the process to transfer. Once at Michigan, he did not want to join a fraternity, but I still wanted to go on hayrides. So he pledged a no-hazing fraternity at Michigan, Sigma Nu, and was eventually elected president (Commander in Sigma Nu titles) himself.

HAIL TO THE VICTORS—LEADERS AND BEST (YEARS)

Two years later, when I asked Bob to ask the Sigma Nus to carry in their national sister sorority, Alpha Xi Delta, they did not turn him or me down. Putting the Chi Omega chapter on top, bringing Sigma Kappa to campus and re-colonizing Alpha Xi Delta gave me a taste for something that I learned that I loved and at which I would learn to excel; getting large groups of people to do difficult things.

HOW MY SORORITY EXPERIENCE INFLUENCED MY CAREER PATH

My leadership style is to embrace what was formerly thought of impossible and inspire others to do it with me. I have learned to aim for the stars, because by reaching only the clouds, it still feels like a win. Whether it is creating a new reputation for your sorority, fighting redistricting for your local elementary school, or raising the awareness of a fifty-year old nonprofit, each journey begins with a single step but good leaders need lots of believers to work alongside them. I've learned to use humor and communication to motivate and inspire others to follow my lead.

Employers recruiting at the University of Michigan loved these skills too. In fact, Procter and Gamble, Macy's, Xerox and other employers especially loved the University of Michigan and their on-campus leaders. In the 1980s, many

Michigan grads were first-generation college students, working to pay for part of their expenses with an amazing work ethic and strong drive to succeed. I hope they still are.

When a close friend and sorority sister, Julie Swain, was headed out one night to attend Macy's wine and cheese open house, I tagged along, strictly for the wine and cheese. There I met Pat Pinardo, a college recruiter who talked me into joining their slate of interviews the next day afer hearing that I was the Panhellenic president, a member of Adara and past Chi Omega president. Before I knew it, I had an offer to join Macy's vaunted executive training program, branded the "Harvard of Retailing." Why not? After all, I was graduating from Michigan, the "Harvard of the Midwest." I accepted the offer and we made plans to head to Atlanta.

Bob and I both loved our Michigan years passionately. We recently went to Houston to watch our Wolverines win the national championship in football in January 2024, as we did at the Rose Bowl in 1998. We reunited with friends that we have not seen in nearly thirty years and it was as if no time had passed.

CHOOSING YOUR PATH

I also learned from my time in Ann Arbor, which was my first taste of independence, that I got to choose my path for the rest of my life. While you do not choose your childhood, you do get to make most of your choices after that. For me, this ultimately meant choosing whether to be happy or not. I chose not to dwell on my trauma.

While my life might have been better if my mother had not taken her own life, it also could have been much worse. I choose not to romanticize the road not taken. I am aware of mothers who snapped and also killed their children, like Andrea Yates. Living with a mother who constantly struggled with mental health issues might not have been a bed of roses either. I do not romanticize the unknown path not taken. I choose not to be a prisoner of my past, but allow it to shape me for the better with resilience and pride for what I have conquered. I choose to win. Sometimes to a fault, but I'm working on that, too.

Some children wither and literally die when separated from their mothers early. Some children are naturally resilient and thrive. Scientists have attempted to study this and still cannot make a distinction as to the "why" as there does not seem to be a gene marker or scientific predictor. While I do not know why as an infant I did not wither, nor why at some point, I chose to thrive. Yet here I am, still making that choice every day.

CHAPTER 4

THE PERFECT(LY AWFUL) MANAGER

AFTER graduation, we moved to Atlanta to begin our careers. Because my offer with Macy's was in Atlanta, it seemed like a great opportunity for Bob and I to start fresh. The late 1980s were not a great time to be in the Midwest economically and my family turmoil seemed like a good thing from which to distance myself. While I had a good relationship with everyone in my family, the same was not true among the rest of them individually. As a result, I often played the role of mediator and peacemaker which put me in a no-win situation that I was happy to escape.

Bob and I chose not even to have a wedding, we just got in the car and drove South. When I think about either of our own children doing this today, I would be devastated, but that thought never crossed my mind in 1986.

As for the lack of a wedding, eventually we rectified that. Bob's mom and dad were headed to Florida and were not thrilled that we were cohabiting in Atlanta out of wedlock and thus were not planning on blessing our arrangement by way of a visit. Apparently they did not understand just how impoverished we were at the time. The idea of each of us having a household was not economically possible, not even remotely.

So, we did what seemed logical to us at the time. We were married by a retired navy chaplain in Marietta and then returned to our apartment located on the wrong side of Atlanta to our rescue puppy, Victor (as in "Hail to the Victors"). Victor was a basset lab mix who looked like a black lab cut off at the knees. He was our first "child" and we loved him dearly.

We called Bob's mom and let her know we were married and they could now come and visit. She seemed relieved and we've made it through thirty-eight years of a largely happy marriage, so we must have done something right. Everyone has their *salad* days, but ours were especially lean.

THE PERFECT (LY AWFUL) MANAGER

A NEW START IN ATLANTA

Our first month in Atlanta was at the Clermont Lodge, a weekly rental *establishment*. I think it's best not to know what might have been going on in the other rooms in this *enterprise* as I am pretty sure that Bob and I were one of the few guests that weren't paying by the hour.

I remember watching Jack Nicklaus win the Masters in 1986 with Bob, and we celebrated his win going to Po' Folks for fried chicken. (For the uninitiated, Po' Folks was a Southern family restaurant chain whose name, which would assuredly not pass today's sensitivity standards, was seemingly on the nose for its clientele). That was a big treat back then. Things have changed a great deal for us in thirty years when it comes to how we celebrate with meals and wine, but I don't think any meal ever tasted better.

Bob took a job selling cars so that we could qualify for an actual apartment while I waited for my training program to start and played stay-at-home mom to our puppy. Eventually, Bob went back to school to become a teacher and coach, while I started at Macy's. At Macy's I learned the basics of merchandising, people management and how to manage a P&L. Everything that I learned at Macy's was very much by-the-book, which was probably not a great thing for a perfectionist-in-training, but it was all I knew. I put it all into practice for many years, which did not make for the most empathetic or flexible manager. I was high performing, rapidly promoted and called it like I saw it. Looking back, though, I would not have wanted to work for my previous self in the earliest years of my career.

Additionally, I was a Midwesterner newly placed in the South. Not only did I have my retail training classmates asking me to repeat words like "wash" and "pop" (which they called soda), I also had to begin a lifelong habit of adding extra words to my writing and speaking. "Abrupt" became my middle name. I am a direct person in general. But take my perfectionist, Midwestern self, and put her in the South and you have abrupt on steroids and it didn't translate well, especially at first.

DEALING WITH DOUBLE STANDARDS

I probably spent hundreds of hours going back and adding extra niceties to emails or words to documents to make them *friendlier*. Part of it is my personal style of directness and part of it is regional communication. However, in 2013 after I read Sheryl Sandberg's book *Lean In*, I learned that it wasn't just geographic or personal style. I learned there really is a double standard in the world, and I have been judged more harshly than my male peers.

I can't tell you how freeing it was to read *Lean In* and learn that I am not the only woman that struggles with these sort of double standards. Men who are direct are aggressive go-getters, while women are referred to as a *bitch*. These days, that is changing, albeit gradually. We did a *Lean In* group book study at HoneyBaked, at the request of some of our female leaders, and they actually told *me* that they recognized my situation in the book. After reading the book, they said that they realized that the previous COO, who had been a hard driving man, got away with a lot more than I did as a less abrasive version of him, without being labeled or resisted.

This same former leader once told me that I used my big smile, sweet face, and blond sisterly looks as a weapon that encouraged others to underestimate me. Then I opened my mouth and "cut them off at the knees". This was definitely before I turned the corner, both in my career and leadership style. I also can't take responsibility for what others assume about me as a blonde female leader. However, I do think that I have been underestimated repeatedly and consistently throughout my career, usually to my advantage.

I also worked longer and harder than the next guy or female too. When I say that I worked eighteen-hour days and six-day weeks many times in my career, I am not exaggerating. I learned that I have a propensity toward workaholism and Macy's took full advantage of that. I also did not know what I was expecting when I completed the "Harvard of Retailing's" six-week program in the downtown Macy's executive headquarters, but it was definitely anything but what I walked into at the Lenox Mall.

I've mentored young people early in their career who are considering opportunities with renowned employers, but hesitate based upon their reviews on Glassdoor as "demanding" or lacking work-life balance in their training program. This makes me chuckle. You can do anything you want in life, but you can't do it all at once. Your first few jobs out of college are your chance to make a great impression, establish yourself and soak up the learning. Working extra is learning extra. Say yes to extra projects. Say thank you for being given an opportunity to do more and see more. It means they *see* more in *you*. Take your vacation and avoid burnout but don't expect a forty-hour week in your first career role.

At Macy's, I, personally, remember hoping that I would be placed out of town, perhaps in a small town like Macon or Augusta where I could be away from the constant attention and criticism of the buyers/merchants. However, Macy's had other plans for me. Apparently that Michigan education and my natural leadership shone through and I was placed at their flagship store, Macy's Lenox Mall, their highest volume store located in Buckhead, home to most of the buyers and senior executives. Yikes!

I was given the Boys and Toddlers department to manage and my saving grace was that my partner manager of infant and girls, Betsy, was a recent North Carolina Tar Heel graduate who was president of her Zeta Tau Alpha sorority. We were so alike that we were nicknamed the "Velcro Twins" because we were always together. Betsy was my first "WBF" (work best friend), but not my last.

Gallup reports that workers are much happier when they have a close friend at work. I have definitely found that to be true everywhere I have worked. Betsy and I sludged through our daily grind, often in tears from a truly toxic work environment mostly fueled by mean-spirited buyers whom we were convinced ate their own young.

(Come to think of it, I never did see anyone with offspring, and I did run the toddler department. Just saying..)

We also suffered severe fatigue as we made our way from our stock rooms to our sales floor and back. This glamorous job billed as the Harvard of retailing was physically demanding and so diverse that any day might include getting a child's shoe lace out of the escalator before they were sucked in, evicting a person experiencing homelessness from the Macy's cellar bathroom or cleaning up a mess in the yogurt area. My area also included the yogurt stand with the highest sales per square foot in the store, thank you very much!

Toward the end of the first year, both "Pretty Betsy," coined by Dave the custodian, and I resorted to walking around with our resignation letters on our persons. This was in case the day got so bad that either of us wanted to quit after hearing our pager signal go off over the sound system one too many times.

The day I reported to Lenox, I met my team of associates Sylvia, Maryland, Sharon, Valerie and a few other part-time employees. They taught me everything that I needed to learn to make the department run. They knew they would still be there when I left, yet they took me under their wings and guided me gently through the daily routines.

When Maryland got pregnant and returned home to have her baby, I went several weeks filling in on the sales floor until I was finally given a blessing from above—Carolyn Morton as a full-time sales associate. Macy's was on commission and Carolyn immediately adopted the Boys Polo department, which I happily assigned to her. Carolyn had recently been subject to the recession of the mid-1980s and was grossly overqualified.

On Carolyn's first evaluation, I had to find some area of opportunity to give her to work on. I meekly asked her to work on her accessory sales and sell a few more socks with each transaction. She nodded and smiled. I returned from a long weekend to find the sock wall empty. I asked her to please fill it in, surprised she had let something like this slip. She slyly said she could not as she had sold every sock in the department and had gone to the young men's department and sold theirs also. Point made.

To this day, Carolyn, Betsy and I still do regular lunches and are great friends. We were in Betsy's wedding and at Carolyn's dad's funeral recently. Working as a junior executive at Macy's is very hard work and it bonds people together. We are definitely friends for life, and it taught me the importance of having close friends and supporters in every job I've had.

One day, about nine months into my sales management assignment, I learned that two of my fellow male sales managers had been promoted to downtown headquarters positions. Both of these gentlemen were great guys but not nearly as well thought of as managers as Betsy and I were—nor were their departments higher performing. I was frankly dumbfounded that they were chosen to be promoted. I got up my nerve and took my ready-made resignation letter out of my pocket and headed down to my store manager's office and laid it on the table and told him that I quit. Mr. Grunwald, which is what all we "junior executives" called him, asked me to sit down and tell him my plans.

This did not take long because I had exactly zero plans beyond quitting. He asked me why I was quitting, and I told him that there were several reasons including the fact that the buyers were mean, that the two guys had just been promoted were less talented and that I hated my job.

In hindsight, he must have been laughing at my twenty-four-year old immaturity, but he never let it show. He wisely advised me that I needed to raise my hand and ask for opportunities to advance or people are never going to give up their best managers willingly. He told me that he was going to give all of my buyers a serious talking to about being mean to me and the other sales managers. Meanwhile, he had a great new opportunity for me: Fashion Accessories and Hosiery.

IF YOU DON'T STAND UP FOR YOURSELF, NO ONE ELSE WILL

I have used this lesson often since then. I spoke up and received a stock option package when I found out that I didn't have the same package as another man at Circuit City. I have used it to get titles and raises and other compensation and benefits and promotions that I deserved many times in my life. Waiting for others to see you doing hard work and promoting you because you deserve it is *a bad* plan. You *must* advocate for yourself or you will toil with your nose to the grindstone until you are resentful and burnt out.

I felt the same way about networking, it was unnecessary, until another WBF, Jo Ann Herold and I, decided to have a LinkedIn contest one weekend. I used to believe that networking was just for finding a new job and I didn't think I needed to waste my time networking either. WRONG! Networking saves me so much time problem solving and learning from others. When Jo Ann and I both decided to see how quickly we could add 500 LinkedIn connections one weekend when we were away on a retreat to the Canyon Ranch, somebody reported to our boss, Chuck Bengochea, that we were at risk of leaving. This was not true, but it is a helpful lesson. LinkedIn is a vital tool in a young person's tool kit. Even when you are working hard, paying your dues and learning a lot, you should never be too busy to invest in yourself, network, and to advocate for yourself. Fullstop.

Back to Mr. Grunwald and my resignation, since I didn't really have a plan, I allowed him to talk me into trying the new department, which was really stupid because I lost my best work friend, something I have now learned is vital to work happiness. I went upstairs to my new department, increased sales, reduced turnovers and shrink, and told them that I wanted to go into Human Resources at the earliest opportunity. They told me if I would just get them through one more holiday (Christmas), they would move me to work for Pat Pinardo, my original mentor, in Human Resources again.

So, I did but not before I got the store ready for one more post-Christmas visit from Mr. Finklestein, the CEO from New York City. After working eighty-hour weeks for the holidays, we gave up our days off to convert the store from holiday merchandise to cruise-wear ready and cleaned everything up for a visit from the very top.

I remember standing on the aisle proudly waiting for "Mr. F." to arrive and inspect my team's work. It was 5pm on a Friday when Lou Schwab, a seasoned department manager, walked by and asked me what I was still doing there. When I told her I was waiting for Mr. Finklestein to see my department, she couldn't stop herself from bursting out laughing.

"Oh sweetie, you fell for the oldest clean up the store after Christmas trick in the book. Finklestein flew out at 3 p.m."

All of the veins in my body contracted and I immediately suffered an excruciating migraine. Bob had to come and pick me up because I could not see out of my right eye. I would not fall for that one again, nor would I ever use it on anyone else. It was the equivalent of retail hazing. He was never coming to our store, but I didn't know that.

MY EARLY DAYS AS A DEMANDING MANAGER

While I was a stellar performer for Macy's, I was not a great person for whom to work. I was a by-the-book manager. I took what I learned in my Macy's training as the absolute truth, and I rarely deviated.

If an associate called in with a sick child, I did not hesitate to advise them that they needed to find better back up child care. If an associate called in because their car wouldn't start, regardless of their financial situation, I would recommend that they find more reliable transportation. Even when I was in HR at the employment desk at Macy's when applicants would come up to apply for a job and ask for a pen to complete the application, I would make sure they knew that it was problematic to come to apply for a job without their own writing utensil. I did this every single time, to every single applicant. Why?

I felt it was my calling to educate the workforce on how

to be better. If it was the truth, I felt it was okay for me to say it. The world had been hard on me and had shared little empathy with me, so I had little to give in return. I regret this immensely now. I remember when my boss and mentor, Mark Arensmeyer, imparted wisdom on me that was truly profound to me. He said, "You know Maggie, just because something is true, doesn't mean you have to say it out loud." Honestly, that thought had never crossed my mind before that the truth should not be said, as stupid as that sounds.

Chuck Bengochea has a slightly more elegant way of saying the same thing to me. He would say, "Perhaps that should have remained a private thought." It took me a long time to rein in my brutal honesty and it is a fine line that I still walk. Having an honest conversation is something that many people struggle with in the business world. Having an honest and direct conversation while maintaining someone else's self-esteem is a truly powerful gift.

I expected perfectionism of myself and everyone around me. A few years later, I had moved on in my career and was the HR Manager at the Belk SouthPark flagship store in Charlotte, North Carolina. I was the senior executive on duty the night before Hurricane Hugo was predicted to hit land in Charleston, 200 miles away. As associates began to call out, the switchboard operator let me know that we weren't going to have enough people to open the store in the morning because of callouts based on the hurricane coming to Charleston.

I volunteered to take over the switchboard and advise associates to not be hasty in their decision making. I distinctly remember chiding the cosmetics associates who were especially alarmed at the impending storm to not worry about a hurricane landing in Charleston, for goodness sake. It struck me as ridiculous that these ladies, known in the retail industry as the prima donnas of the trade, were worried about a hurricane in Charlotte, North Carolina, a four-hour drive from the coast.

God has quite a sense of humor, as mere hours later, at 4 a.m., I was quaking in my pajamas holding on to the bathtub of my rented townhome as Hugo, now a tropical storm, roared through Charlotte. I remember praying that the roof of my townhome did not get sucked off with me under it. When it was finally light, Charlotte looked like it had snowed leaves everywhere on the streets and lawns. There were National Guardsmen on major corners with automatic weapons directing traffic. I had no power and would not get any power restored for over a week. That taught me.

As I walked to the store from my nearby home the next morning, I saw a few executives there, including Tim

Belk, one of the owners of the chain. He pulled me aside and asked how I was. I told him that I was fine but a little embarrassed as I told most everyone that it would be fine to come in to work today. He had already heard that and gave me the gentlest, kindest lecture about always letting adults make their own decisions about prioritizing their family, safety and work, in that order. I'd love to say that this lecture stuck, but it took a few more years and having a family of my own before I really understood that work will never come before a mother's love of her children or the safety of her family. Nor should it.

After Belk, I went to work for Circuit City stores in multi-unit HR management. These were the glory days of Circuit City and a great job where I had several amazing mentors and worked on an incredible team. It was also a commissioned sales culture with a rough-and-tumble culture, but our Executive Vice President Bill Zierden created a culture where HR didn't just have a seat at the table—we were respected business partners before it was a standard business practice.

I was in my early thirties in a male-dominated culture, but I adapted and thrived. I was even able to teach the guys a little about feminism and learned some things along the way. I worked for Mark Arensmeyer as my HR boss and Pete Douglas as my operational boss, and then Mike Froning as Southern Division President. We grew, developed, and promoted more than anyone in the company. We were known for exporting talent and we all loved that part of our jobs and we were an amazing team. Zierden was constantly trying to study how we did it to recreate it elsewhere, but it was lightning in a bottle with our team. Mark, Pete and I were aligned on the importance of people to performance and it showed.

That did not, however, always extend to the entire field and HR values. I remember coming back from a store-opening trip on the Florida Panhandle and complaining to Arensmeyer that after dinner the guys had dropped Charlotte, the store manager, and me off at the hotel. They'd then gone out to the "shoe show." I told him that, "It made me mad because Charlotte and I probably like shoes more than they do."

His jaw dropped and he was incredulous that I was so naive to not really know where they were going. When he told me what a "shoe show" actually was —where the women are *only* wearing shoes— I tried to retract telling him, but that was not possible. If I had known, I'm not sure I would have told my boss about the incident as opposed to discussing it with the group myself as there were several senior-level executives in the group. I thought I was just whining about being left off a shopping trip. Turns out I got some people in serious trouble which was not my intent.

Even though Circuit, as we called it, was largely male, the HR team was full of great female leaders who had to learn how to influence without direct authority and we did. I had some great work best friends there; Debbie Sharp and Cindy Batey, that made the job a joy but we also competed like crazy for annual awards. The culture was unique and something that Zierden should be very proud of for having created such a unique people culture.

I thrived at Circuit City, opening scores of stores in St. Louis, Chicago (where we briefly moved), Minneapolis and then returning to Atlanta. When I left Circuit City in 2002, shortly after the birth of my first son and the terrorist attack of September 11, 2001, I thought that I was going to nest for a while, but God had another plan that led me to an amazing opportunity with Honey Baked Ham and even more so with Chuck Bengochea. Chuck taught me about being a servant leader and a mentor in a way that very few could.

Chuck Bengochea, Mark Arensmeyer, Pat Pinardo, Bill Zierden, Pete Douglas, Mike Frongin, Dave Keil, Doug Higgins, Russ Grunwald, Bill Brigham are just a few of the amazing mentors who have invested in me and saw potential beyond the rough-around-the-edges talent. I'm not sure if they picked me or I chose them but they have put their thumb prints on my career indelibly. Thank you all and to those not named but who have made their mark and allowed me to help you along the way.

Mentors are worth their weight in gold and I don't think enough companies appreciate how important they are to retention and happiness. I have also tried to be a good mentor and it is a joy to give back by mentoring. I hope that this next generation of talent will turn around and help the next person up as well. It's a great tradition, it is good for business and it's good for your soul.

CHAPTER 5

(SCAR-BASED) LEADERSHIP

PROBABLY based upon my less-than-ideal early childhood (ya think?) I battled depression for most of my adult life. However, it wasn't until our first dog Victor died at age eight that I had a mini-meltdown.

We were living in Chicago and I am not exaggerating by a day when I say that I worked 364 days that year opening eighteen Circuit City stores in the Chicago area. I can't remember which day I actually took off—I think it was Easter. I had lived away from Bob for six months, it was a bitterly cold winter, and I leaned heavily into my workaholism. We thought we were going to be closer to family and friends but we had little opportunity to see either. Once Bob and I settled together, we ended up building a home in the far northwest suburbs.

When Victor died suddenly, it threw me into a nosedive mentally. It was another instance of life being really unfair. Pets have been an important source of unconditional love throughout my life. I really felt that I had paid life's sadness toll by age seventeen and that the really bad stuff should be behind me. I also suffered lifelong separation anxiety, so losing a dog was like losing a family member—and losing a beloved dog at a mere eight years old was more than unfair to me. I let God know that I did not appreciate it. I recovered after a weeklong crying jag and some time of healing, but I was still emotionally fragile.

But then, infertility hit and everything finally caught up with me—a lifetime of shame, blame and anger. We had moved back to Atlanta and this time I was *very* angry with God. I didn't understand how much He could expect me to take. In truth, in the early years of our marriage, we didn't think we wanted children, or rather I didn't and Bob went along with me. I don't think I wanted to repeat my pain. I remember even saying things like I was afraid our baby might have red hair (like my mother) or what if the

(SCAR-BASED) LEADERSHIP

baby had colic?

How is that for maternal and self-loathing?

Bob said it didn't matter to him if we couldn't have children, but it did to me. I even told him that we should divorce if it turned out that I really couldn't have children after exploring all options, because I was so certain that *he* would be a great dad (and he is). I saw our Episcopal priest at the time, but he wasn't terribly helpful. In all truthfulness, nobody was going to be helpful if they didn't deliver a baby.

But my prayers were something like, "I understand you took my mom, my dad, and my favorite dog, but I can't have a child, GOD? Really? What did I ever do to you? You owe me a child." I really did feel that a child would be a source of unconditional love that had been missing in my life.

OUR JOURNEY WITH IVF

After rounds of testing, our fertility specialist, nicknamed Dr. Gloom and Doom, told us that I had high follicle-stimulating hormone (FSH). In other words, my eggs were too old but we could try intrauterine insemination (IUI) five times because "it was our money to waste."

It's a wonder he chose fertility specialist as his occupation and not motivational speaking.

His rationale was that we had a 1 percent chance of success because of my advanced maternal age, which was a whopping thirty-seven years old. After five rounds, we would need to move on to donor eggs or adoption. They would not do more than five because it was emotionally draining to fail more than five times. I did not plan to fail at all. I **never** plan to fail.

In July 2000, we tried our first cycle. We had a mixed doubles tennis match that morning that my tests said was the optimal time. Never one to want to miss a match, Bob dropped off his "package" and went to play tennis with his alternate partner. I followed shortly behind him for the procedure. Later that day we headed home to Michigan for a vacation. My cycle was late while we were there and I could not wait. I had to know. I had the faintest of lines but there was definitely a line, and it was positive.

We learned in Michigan that we were finally expecting—the 1 percent chance had happened. The first miracle of this pregnancy had occurred, but not the last. I had been ceaselessly praying as well as taking wheatgrass and various other holistic cures, but I really believe it was the prayers. I literally begged God for a child.

On March 27, 2001, Riley Joseph Michaels DeCan was born by emergency C-section after attempting to be induced twelve hours earlier. It took a few hours for me to recover to the point that I could even hold him but around 10 p.m. that evening, Bob came with tears in his eyes, as he put our son in my arms. Bob said thank you for pushing to have our baby, you were so right. I just smiled.

As Bob handed Riley to me, I heard God speak to me as clearly as if he were standing right next to me. God said to me, "Your mother loves you this much. I love you more." At that moment, I experienced the peace that passes all understanding.

I immediately understood that she was ill and did not leave me. I understood in a new way that nobody who is not ill leaves this kind of love. I did not need to forgive her anymore than I needed to forgive my dad for having a heart attack after being diagnosed with Type II diabetes and continuing to eat ice cream. The shame, the anger and everything else was washed away with my son's birth and God's boundless love.

This encounter with the Divine and the birth of my son and the love that filled my heart changed me profoundly. By this time, I was the head of HR for the billion-dollar Southern Division of Circuit City Stores. Someone wise told me that I was setting an example for other women who would either take their maternity leave or not, based on me, so I took my leave and did not even return emails while I was out. I enjoyed my time with my son. I remember spending an entire day in a glider just holding him, wanting to cherish every minute with him. I did the same with Brady when he was born. I cherish those days.

Even before I left on leave, I was still very independent, wanting to be in control of myself and ask nothing of anyone. My division president, Michael Froning, came to me to tell me that everyone was so happy that we were going to finally have a baby that they were dying to have a shower for me, and he had heard that I refused. I told him that I felt uncomfortable having people who were making far less than me give me gifts that we could afford to purchase. He told me that I didn't get it, and he ordered me to be "showered." It is harder to receive than to give.

He was so right. It was a glorious shower, and I learned so much that day about sharing your joy with others and allowing others to celebrate with you.

RETURNING TO WORK

When I returned to work, life was different, work was different, and priorities were different. Riley's baptism was scheduled for September 16, 2001. On Tuesday, September 11, 2001, the terrorists struck America. Riley's baptism was

(SCAR-BASED) LEADERSHIP

delayed until November. We reprinted his baptismal invitation with the quote, "A baby is God's proof that life should go on." In a strange omen we served a Honey Baked Ham to mark the specialness of the occasion. I ordered his Christening gown from England, and my heart was literally bursting as he was baptized at St. James Church in Marietta. My cup and gratitude to God literally overflowed that Sunday surrounded by family and friends. It was my own celebration and thanksgiving to God in one party.

A few months later, Circuit City decided to close down its most profitable and successful Southern division in Atlanta as it slowly drove itself from *Good to Great to Gone*, which is also chronicled in Alan Wurtzel's 2016 book. I was offered an opportunity to move to Richmond, take a lesser role in Atlanta, or exercise my employment contract.

Thank goodness for those "employment contracts" that guarantee you paid severance in return for not going to work for the competitor. I took the contract and planned to nest with Riley for a year when a recruiter from Korn Ferry called with an HR leadership opportunity with Honey Baked Ham. I did some research and learned that HoneyBaked, under Chuck Bengochea, was a unique company with a very values-focused culture.

When I drove across the northern suburbs of Atlanta to

interview with my future boss Chuck, who was the COO at the time, and President Kent Smith, it was quite a unique experience. Kent was sitting yoga-style on the floor stretching. He would ask me Harvard MBA-type questions like, "Explain the value proposition of the commission sales person at Circuit City." Chuck would then translate from his chair, and I would answer to both of them. It was one of the strangest interviews I've ever experienced.

I left thinking that there was no way I was going to hear from them again, but I did.

Next visit, I interviewed with the CEO and owner, Linda Farbolin van Rees, the granddaughter of the founder of HoneyBaked and the inventor of the spiral slicer. Our conversation was so authentic. She spoke of wanting more women working in the field and senior leadership. She was brilliant and very strategic. Ironically, as a seasoned retailer, I did not get many typical retail questions. HoneyBaked saw itself more as a brand than a retailer, something that we would wrestle with in the future.

She also asked me about my son Riley and if I planned on having any more. I loved that she delved into questions that most executives felt were off-limits. I told her that I didn't think I would with starting a new job. She said "Don't wait because of this." She definitely had me with that sage advice.

When offered the job at HoneyBaked, I accepted readily. On the whole, everyone was so kind and authentic, and my contact with the yoga stretching, floor-sitting leader turned out to be very limited. As it turned out, he was gone soon after I joined and instead Chuck Bengochea was made the first non-family member CEO, while I was soon promoted to Vice President of Human Resources. I became Chuck's right hand and we worked together closely for twelve years.

Given Linda's encouragement and HoneyBaked's infertility health coverage, we quickly pursued our second miracle, to which Dr. Denis was even more skeptical, but again, we did not plan to fail.

This time, due to my even more advanced age of thirty-nine, Dr. Denis told me that I could only try Clomid and IUI three times, to which I quickly agreed. Again, God blessed us on the very first cycle. Indeed, it was twins but only one embryo actually made it over six weeks. While sad, we were overjoyed at our second miracle from God.

Brady Robert Michaels DeCan was born in June 2003. I remember wondering as I packed for the hospital how I could ever love a baby more than I loved Riley, but I soon wondered how I could ever imagine life without both of my amazing boys. Our family was complete, and my heart seemed fully healed as we looked to move to Roswell, the halfway point between HoneyBaked and Etowah High School, where Bob taught economics and coached tennis.

LEADERSHIP LESSONS FROM CHUCK

Meanwhile, I was so blessed at HoneyBaked to work for Chuck, who was one of the best mentors anyone could ever have at work or in life. Not only did he teach me about real servant leadership—and it took every one of our twelve years together for it to really sink in—he taught me great lessons about faith, marriage, parenting, and life. He and I didn't always see eye-to-eye, but I always respected him and always listened.

In turn, he always listened. His super power was coaching in such an elegant manner that sometimes it would take hours for you to understand that he actually coached you, rather than complimented you.

Sometimes as his HR leader, it was my job to translate for others that were less able to understand his elegance that he actually coached them when they didn't really hear what he was saying. Chuck was a firm believer that whenever there was a disconnect between two members of a team, the senior member of the team should own it and was responsible for fixing the issue. I have repeated this advice to myself, used it, and repeated it to others more times than I could count. So many senior leaders feel like position means that others need to bend to them, but that is the opposite. Real leadership means that you, as the leader, are charged with helping the associate struggling with childcare, transportation or worrying about a pending storm. If Chuck had been my supervisor earlier in my career, I would have been a better leader sooner.

Chuck was also an amazing listener. I think that part of this had to do with early hearing loss in one ear so he had to listen closely, but he also cared deeply about what his team members were trying to communicate with him. He would make sure that we sat on the side of his "good" ear in our one-on-one meetings. He often would repeat back his own translation of what he heard me say to make sure that he was really internalizing what he heard.

And while Chuck is a biblical scholar and an evangelical Christian, at work he was gender blind and always pushing me out of my comfort zone trying to get me to take on more responsibility. However, knowing my predisposition toward workaholism, I didn't want to take on a role that would require too much time away from our young sons early in their lives, so I kept declining Chuck's requests to go too far beyond HR (although I did take on Real Estate, Administration and a few ancillary duties).

BALANCING RESPONSIBILITIES AS BUSINESS LEADER AND MOTHER

As I took on more responsibility, one of the tools that I had at my disposal was a secret weapon, Stephanie Stephenson—our nanny, house manager, and amazing support system for us. Stephanie eased my working mother's guilt and made Bob's and my life easier. She would shop for birthday gifts for upcoming parties to which the kids were invited and make sure that the family calendar was running smoothly. She would also make sure that my kids never looked like they had a mom who wasn't paying attention.

In first grade, she left a spelling test from Riley on the counter with a sticky note with a frown on it. Riley had scored 100 so I had to dig in to see that his spelling words were *dog, cat* and *boy*. Much too simple for him. I'm not sure that Riley appreciated that Mrs. Stephenson's prompt got him his own language arts curriculum and his spelling words were soon *tarantula* and *chrysanthemum*.

Stephanie also understood that I didn't want my kids to ever appear to be less loved than the kids whose moms stayed home and did the hard work of raising children all day. So one

(SCAR-BASED) LEADERSHIP

day when the room mother from Mrs. Huber's class called to tell me that it was my turn to provide the snack for the field trip to the teaching museum, I willingly agreed. However, when she continued with, "Mrs. Huber was thinking that Rice Krispie treats would be good, so would that be okay?" I was still agreeable. However when she closed with "Now, I know you work and will buy them, so let's plan for two per child because the store-bought ones are small." I fumed as I hung up the phone and called Stephanie to rant.

All I can say is that those handmade, M&M-filled Rice Krispy treats that each child got that day, individually wrapped in colored Saran Wrap and tied with hand tied curling ribbon were as big as frisbees. I am quite sure that Mrs. Huber did not appreciate the sugar high that accompanied each child back from the teaching museum but it's not my fault that my snack-providing mothering skills were challenged. As for whether Stephanie or I made them, that is a secret that the two of us will take to our graves.

While my snack skills might have been outsourced, I more than carried my own weight when it came to pitching in at school. The school district decided that our beloved Roswell North Elementary was going to be part of a redistricting in 2007 and 2008. According to all sources, it was a done deal and the bus drivers were already learning their new routes and we were going to lose one of our biggest, most involved and affluent neighborhoods.

Not so fast, my friends, to quote College GameDay's legendary Lee Corso.

I met with my, now, dear friend, Jerome Huff, the principal of the world's best elementary school. Jerome, who was always an optimist, indicated that he thought it was pretty much a done deal, as well. This was not okay with me.

I learned all there was to know about the process of soliciting input from the community and then rallying it. I started a newsletter that used my humor and writing skills to inform everyone about important dates and talking points. By the end of the process, I had over 700 readers opt in to my ad hoc email. We made our point that we loved our school's mix where about one-third of the families have enough to share, one-third of the families have all they need, and one-third could use a little help and how that works for us.

After the first round of proposals showed no possibility of the big neighborhood going anywhere else, we were all united on keeping RNE exactly the same and we showed out at every meeting. In the final meeting, other schools got their attorney's involved and attempted to threaten legal action to keep the county from adding more diversity to

(SCAR-BASED) LEADERSHIP

their school. We stood up and proudly told Fulton County Schools that we loved our diversity just the way it is. Fulton County Schools did not change a single thing about our district lines, and I became a bit of a folk hero at RNE.

People would stop me in the halls of school and thank me for my efforts and even ask me, "I heard you work?" and I would say yes, that's true, it just requires me to be more organized and sleep a bit less.

The PTA that originally took no position on redistricting nominated me for the state of Georgia PTA's highest award, Visionary Leadership. I was so honored to win it that summer as Jerome was also honored for his leadership. Any award that was won by anyone at RNE was highly celebrated by us all. We all love that little school.

While I am so proud of my contributions to Roswell North Elementary and not at all embarrassed about the Rice Krispy treats or some of my other antics, there are a few things that I look back on with regret where I took financial shortcuts that make me cringe now. The main one is Boosterthon.

For those of you that have never experienced the thrill of participating in a Boosterthon Fun Run event in your elementary school, it is a pyramid marketing campaign that turns a typical kindergartner into a Zig Zigler of sales marketing—all designed to earn them Boosterthon Swag like water bottles and key chains. The more you raise, the more you earn.

However, much like the baby shower or asking my mom to pack my lunch, I was not a big fan of asking people to pay money to my children's elementary school. (This is quite the plot twist from the current CEO of the Children's Development Academy, whose most important responsibility is fundraising). At the time, I was making a handsome salary, but I also wanted my childrens' school to get the money and I didn't want my boys to feel left out. So I stroked a check. Yep, I stroked a check on the first day of the campaign for the full amount for both boys to ensure that both the boys would get the maximum prizes possible. A couple of parents did mention to me that their children were jealous of the boys getting all the prizes on the first day, but it didn't really register back then.

It registers now as I deal with families every day who have so little. In the quest for efficient execution, I was really thoughtless. Looking back now, I'm sorry and embarrassed. Even though through the rest of the year, I would never send in a single check for my kids without also paying for another child who might not be able to attend a field trip or buy supplies, when it came to Boosterthon, I was over the top.

LEANING INTO YOUR SCARS

In the fall of 2009, I took over the corporate and franchise stores on my way to becoming Chief Operating Officer. Part of that journey involved a personal metamorphosis. Always a tough manager, I evolved and grew under Chuck, but always with high standards. Running a business that does over 60 percent of its revenue on less than twenty days of the year requires a lot of focus.

In case you missed that, I'm going to say that again. I ran a business that did over 60 percent of its revenue on only 20 working days a year. Oh yeah and sometimes, there are blizzards during the winter on a few of those days in your biggest markets. That is high stakes, very challenging, and requires a lot of planning and attention to detail. You literally cannot leave anything to chance.

I took a different approach than had been used in the past and was different than was expected from "Maggie from HR." As a life long, classically trained retailer, it was the norm to have store visits, pre-holiday visits and certain detailed inspections. But these were not part of the culture at HoneyBaked. I was also habitually working late hours and sending emails at 2 a.m. I didn't really embrace the argument that if I was sending them, people thought I expected them to answer them in real time. But I also loved my managers at HoneyBaked and connected with most of them deeply. I coached them because I cared about them and wanted them to prosper and grow and be the best that they could be.

In 2012, after taking over the stores, introducing a lot of unpopular things like store-visit reports and Holiday Leadership Team inspections, I got a lot of resistance to what I was trying to accomplish. I am not sure that I shared enough of the *why* and the heart behind the initiatives. I felt the need to share myself more fully with each and every manager who worked for me. So, I decided to tell them more about who I was, sharing with them my scars and faults.

So at our summer Store Management Conference at the Ritz Carlton at Lake Oconee, I stood on the stage in the grand ballroom and told them that I was anything but perfect. I told them that I was as much of a screwed-up mess as anyone in the room, probably much more, but I was a work in progress, and I hoped they would work with me.

I told them about losing my mom and finding out about it in the newspaper article. I told them about my dad dying on Christmas Eve unexpectedly. I told them that I tend toward workaholism because I still feel the need

(SCAR-BASED) LEADERSHIP

to justify my place on this earth. I told them the story of Riley's birth and how God's love has definitely healed me, but not totally fixed me. I didn't need to tell them that I was a perfectionist or a control freak. Most of them knew that. I told them that I try to be kinder and gentler, but I cared about them so much, I want them to be great so I have trouble walking by mediocrity. I told them that if even one person was better because of my truth-telling today, it would be worth it.

I did a practice session of my talk while our managers were lunching elsewhere. When I came back, post practice, after taking a break, the Ritz Carlton staff had placed tissue boxes on all the tables. Apparently, the staff who had been setting the lunch tables had cried during my rehearsal and they didn't want the managers using the white napkins for tissues. Talk about attention to detail and leaving nothing unplanned.

I have to say that my talk exceeded all my expectations. There were so many managers who lined up to talk to me afterward and tell me about their scars and imperfections. Being vulnerable and being authentic accelerates trust. I call it scar-based leadership.

Trying to be perfect is outdated and exhausting, especially for women. Teams and individuals want their leader to be real, trustworthy, and authentic. When women try to appear all buttoned up, I think it is even more off-putting to someone who might be expecting nurturing, kindness, or maternal warmth. Most of all, people want authenticity and honesty from their leaders.

When people understand your message, especially if that includes scars, warts and imperfections, it frees them to be more real as well. In this Photoshopped, staged, and highly contoured world, people are craving authenticity. Reality television is anything but real. But realism in the workforce, in relationships, and in dialogues accelerate trust-building. Scar-based leadership is the key to creating real relationships in work and life.

If others trust your intent, if they know your heart, they can forgive you almost all of your oddities. I know that some of my idiosyncrasies can be an acquired taste and that my middle name was "Abrupt" for much of my early career, but most of the people who worked for me understood that my intentions were noble and my high standards were ultimately good for their career.

My talk to my team of 200 general managers changed our relationships, communication and accelerated our trust. It also improved results for our entire company. I think that it is the moment that I decided that my life's work needed

(SCAR-BASED) LEADERSHIP

to be about more than EBITDA and strategy. In the end, it ultimately put me on the path to the CDA and more meaningful work. That talk ultimately led me to write this book and share my story multiple times since then.

I was once on a panel with an incredibly accomplished, young Black woman. We were asked about our approach to leadership. The young woman, whom I believe was an attorney for Delta Air Lines at the time, spoke about the weight she carried being the "first Black woman to do this" and the "first Black woman to do that." She was exceptional and constantly in the spotlight and the pace car for an entire class of women. I spoke next and I think I let out a big sigh before I spoke because I felt so badly for her and the weight of her responsibility exhausted me *for* her.

I felt so badly for the responsibility she carried as my approach is the 180-degree opposite. I told the audience that I try to let people know just how imperfect I am as quickly as possible. I have learned that my mess is an important part of my message. I try to lean into it whenever possible. I do not attempt to be, nor even appear to be, perfect. I relayed that for me, as a leader, the sooner my team knows that I am imperfect, the sooner that they, too, let their guard down and trust will grow.

At this event, I was honored when Carol Tome', then the

CFO at Home Depot and now the CEO at UPS, approached me to share that she enjoyed my answer and hoped that more people would embrace their authentic self as leaders. Wow! Carol Tome' was already a bit of a hero to me as a female leader working in Atlanta. Knowing that she, too, agreed with scar-based leadership, even if she might not call it that, was and is inspiring to me.

So, I continue to implore those I coach, mentor, speak to and readers now, to show your scars. It is also a great gift to grow older and care less and less each year about what others think of you. Leading with your scars and being nearly impervious to other's opinions is a gift worth the wrinkles of life.

Subsequent to my talk at Lake Oconee, I can't tell you how many times I would go into a manager's office and see one of my handwritten cards pinned proudly on their bulletin boards. My CEO Chuck said that because my standards were high, when they got a card from me or a compliment, it meant more. I hope so. I could fill this book with the names of people who have touched my life and made me so proud of being part of the growth of their career as well as those that have helped me along the way. I hope that each of them know the difference they have made in my life. I think they do.

(SCAR-BASED) LEADERSHIP

I have to say that I also collect the cards and letters that I have received that mean a lot to me. I still do. I once heard a CEO say that she had an "I Love Me" file and whenever she was having a tough day, she'd pull it out. In the file were the keepsakes that spoke to her from over the years and it would immediately remind her that this feeling of being attacked or unworthy or of being an imposter was fleeting. It was a great takeaway, and I tell those that I mentor about it frequently.

I encourage everyone to have an "I Love Me" file. Everyone needs to start embracing themself as a leader, loving who they are in all their imperfections. When someone gives us a piece of positive affirmation—in writing—darn right we should save it! Heck, we should laminate it.

CHAPTER 6

THE CDA'S FIRST HARD YEAR (DITCH OF DESPAIR)

AFTER leaving HoneyBaked, I wish that I could say that my transition to the nonprofit world was an easy, breezy piece of cake, but that would be a flat-out lie. It was hard work—mentally, physically, and emotionally. There was some overlap between my tenure and the executive director's whom I was succeeding. This was a blessing in some ways and also a bit frightening at times.

For example, one of the first things that the outgoing executive director suggested to me, as part of my development plan, was to watch Dan Pallotta's TED Talk titled, "The Way

We Think About Charity is Dead Wrong." Pallotta, who was an entrepreneur and humanitarian activist, was the inventor of the multi-day charitable fundraiser, such as the 3-Day Breast Cancer Walk. While events like the 3-Day walk were abruptly canceled when placed under the microscope of the expenses to host as a percentage of funds raised, he was a visionary in expanding the reach and awareness of charitable causes and fundraising.

A CRISIS OF CONFIDENCE IN MY BRAND-NEW ROLE

In his TED Talk, he challenges the morality of this expense-control-first model and asks to consider rewarding charities for bigger achievements, even if they cost more to produce. Notably, he rhetorically ponders if cancer researchers would rather have 90 percent of a lemonade stand or 65 percent of a multimillion dollar, three-day walk. In one of his most memorable points that spoke to me personally—and led to some inner soul-searching—he considers two MBA grads. One goes to work in the private sector, makes significant money, gives to a nonprofit, and eventually chairs the board of the organization to which he donates. The other graduate goes to work for the same nonprofit as the executive director and ends up working for the other classmate.

THE CDA'S FIRST HARD YEAR (DITCH OF DESPAIR)

His example certainly gave me pause on my first day of work. Talk about a crisis of confidence in the first week on the job. Maybe I would have been better off—and the CDA would have been too—if I had listened to Mike, taken the recruiter's other job, joined the CDA's board, and made healthy donations. I certainly could have made healthy donations to the CDA, women's causes, food insecurity, and mental health causes if I had taken the seven-figure job and not fought for the 86 percent pay cut. Why had this been item 1A on my development plan to watch a video that made me question my own choice?

The other provoking question that came to me even before the TED Talk, which I still ponder to this day, is the very word *nonprofit*. Put it in the basket with other nonsensical misnomers like Chinese checkers (actually invented in Germany in 1892), koala bears (technically marsupials), and the Panama hat (woven in Ecuador). It is the absolute opposite of the truth. As an industry, the work that is done in the so-called "nonprofit" sector actually profits everyone; those who work in it, those who are served by it, as well as the community that surrounds and is served by it.

While I understand the P&L implications that there are no dividends to distribute to anyone at the end of the year (hence no profits), the name of the industry could not be more inappropriate. I nearly refused to participate from Day One in calling the CDA a "nonprofit." That said, I lacked, and to this day do not hold, the clout to rename an industry, much less a federal tax classification.

This is my attempt, ever so feeble, to make the case that nonprofit is not the right title for one of the most competitive, hardworking, undercompensated, and necessary components of the American economy. We should do better by it.

TAKING OVER IN MY NEW ROLE

When I took the wheel at the CDA, I was replacing someone who had been at the organization for 14 years and had done an amazing job. Under her leadership, the CDA had become National Association for the Education of Young Children (NAEYC) accredited, which is the gold standard of accreditation in early education. It is the Good Housekeeping seal of approval for early education, but much harder to earn. She moved the school to a new level of quality which is imperative to the population of children we are serving.

However, when I joined, there were some gaps on the team that needed to be filled, especially in facilities. In this situation, a hire was made in part because the outgoing executive director was departing and she wanted me to have a full team. In hindsight, I know that I would not have made that hire. But nonetheless, a man, whom we will call Tommy, was hired and he was unlike anybody that I had personally managed in over twenty-five years. It harkened back to my early days in retail managing hourly employees at Macy's, although the women in the Boys and Toddler department were never caught smoking weed on the property or sleeping on the job. Even though the Macy's department employees were in their forties and I was twenty-two, they were helpful and kind—knowing that in eighteen months a new trainee would rotate through. Tommy was a challenge from the very first day.

Another concern that I had, irrational perhaps but very real, was that the funding tap was going to somehow go dry the minute the incumbent packed up her desk and left. I remember sitting across the desk from her and expressing this concern to which she laughed and tried to assure me that this would not happen as we scoured the P&L to examine all of the revenue streams that were relatively secure and a few that were more variable like events, individual giving and foundations. I was moderately assured, but only just so.

There were so many blessings the first year also, such as North Point Community Church and their Be Rich campaign. It is an amazing endeavor undertaken by this groundbreaking church, led by Pastor Andy Stanley. Every fall North Point raises millions *each year* that goes directly back into the community to support highly vetted organizations selected by North Point to fund specific projects and initiatives. North Point has annually supported the CDA for more than ten years, regularly funding our children's tuition, teacher compensation and other projects to the tune of over $1 million since they have started supporting our organization. To that end, North Point doesn't just write checks—their volunteers are amazing and highly committed and they pray for us and care for us all year. They are obviously our biggest faith partner and one of our biggest funders overall.

It was a very big deal then when I was asked to be on stage for the kickoff of the Be Rich campaign in my very first week on the job. Specifically, it was my second day of work. While I was supposed to go to the lake with my family that weekend, I quickly learned that time and weekends are not my own in this new role, so I rearranged and eagerly accepted the opportunity to make thousands of people aware of the CDA and our mission.

When it came time to talk about the CDA, I shared statistics with the audience from James Heckman, a Nobel Prize winning economist who validated the importance of

THE CDA'S FIRST HARD YEAR (DITCH OF DESPAIR)

high-quality early education for all children, and especially children from low-income households—like those we serve at the CDA. As I explained to the audience, his research showed that children receiving high-quality early education are more likely to be ready for kindergarten, reading by third grade, graduate from high school, attend college, have fewer unplanned pregnancies, less likely to end up in prison, more likely to hold jobs, pay taxes, and even less likely to be divorced and have intact families. The pastor asked me a few more questions, thanked me for spending my first day on the job at North Point, and I returned to my seat.

As I settled back in, an executive director with another local nonprofit leaned over and softly told me that I had just offended half of the people in the audience. I continued to smile on stage and wondered how I had possibly already screwed up so badly less than forty-eight hours into my new role. As the presentation closed, I approached the woman and asked her to explain her comment. She said that half of all marriages in America end up in divorce and I probably didn't want to use not being divorced as a success statistic. I made a mental note of her feedback, although I wasn't yet sure if I was going to delete *intact families* as a measure of success for early childhood although I would probably be careful about the audiences in which I shared it. I thanked her for the coaching.

While the feedback definitely stung, I always appreciate when people care enough to share their opinions. In fact, all of my new peers were very helpful for the first year and beyond. My fellow local nonprofit leaders were incredibly generous with information, sharing deadlines, offering advice, and making sure that I didn't miss anything important. They were also very receptive to helping the new kid on the block, even though I did not have a background in social work or nonprofits. Kathy Swahn at the Drake House, Barbara Duffy at North Fulton Community Charities, Rose Burton of HomeStretch, Holly York of MUST Ministries, and Ameera Joe of North Point Community Church were like a sisterhood that wove itself into a safety net for me. They didn't have to do it and I know they did it for the CDA, the families and children that we serve, and our community as well as me. I'm forever grateful and try to return the favor whenever I can.

Another event that was incredibly positive that first November was a reception that was held to welcome me as the new Executive Director. Originally they were planning to have it in someone's home or in the lovely marble lobby of a local bank, but I suggested that we do it at the CDA in our large West Hall (now Hagan Hall) where the PreK class ate. They did not regularly hold donor events at the school because, frankly, our school is not located in a premier area of

Roswell, not many people knew how to find it, and it wasn't top of mind. But I had already done just enough reading to be dangerous and knew that if you had an asset like a building, you should leverage it.

We held "Roots and Wings" in November and invited board members donors, and a lot of my friends and connections. To this day, I am humbled by how many people showed up. There were other parents from our sons' baseball team, friends from Roswell North Elementary, tennis teammates, and so many other peers. I was touched. When I asked people to raise their hand if they had never been to the CDA before, 90 percent of the hands went up. My friend Dana Moore said it was a brilliant move to demonstrate to the board how many people I had brought in already. But I wasn't that forward thinking. I was just so excited to see how many people we had introduced to our precious and important school.

This event was just the first of many instances where my friends, colleagues and family rallied my new cause and me. They gave their time, talents, and treasures generously and repeatedly. Sometimes, I feel a bit guilty when I text for dollars, or do yet another Facebook appeal with pictures of our children, but so many of my friends give so generously and enthusiastically that I am grateful for their support. It is part of the job and why it is paramount to have a deep belief in your mission because you have to be deeply committed to your cause to ask for support—again, again, and again.

Likewise, you have to live in a perpetual state of gratitude. I do live in an eternal state of gratitude, but you have to make sure that you show *radical* gratitude to each and every donor and it better be genuine or they will sniff it out. They deserve to know they are appreciated. And I am legitimately so grateful for all the amazing support that we received in the first year and continue to receive. Yet it is a theme that I hear from retiring executives that it will be nice to stop genuflecting and living in a constant state of gratitude. I have tried to make part of the CDA's brand equity one of radical gratitude, and we try to demonstrate that. I hope I never lose my joy for thanking people for giving to our kids.

Most donors tell us that we do a pretty good job distinguishing ourselves in this way. Every donor gets a signed thank you letter with a handwritten thank you note from me. I stole this from my national women's fraternity, Chi Omega. Thank you, Sally Kimball. We also use social media and other opportunities to thank others every chance we get. I never want to sound ungrateful at all, but I also understand how it can be emotionally draining to constantly be on the receiving end of a donation. It is much easier and more fun to be the giver than the receiver.

Regardless of whether you are poor or are receiving on behalf of the less fortunate, the giver definitely has the fun. But they also deserve to be genuinely and profusely thanked and shown the impact of their gift. I recently visited a nonprofit that did not practice radical gratitude, in fact, the volunteer leader barely practiced any gratitude. It reinforced for me how correct our strategy of demonstrating radical gratitude is and how important it is to maintain it.

CHANGING CULTURE

My day-to-day work life at the CDA was very interesting. I quickly learned that my predecessor placed great value in what I call "office time." Keeping in mind that this was very much pre-Covid, the former Executive Director and our school's Center Director, who were both salaried, would complete weekly time cards. The primary reason for this, to me, seemed to be to keep track of who worked more hours. On my first day on the job, I announced to our very hard working preschool Center Director that she was the perpetual winner of the weekly hours contest and told everyone that timesheets for salaried employees were no longer required. That went over like a lead balloon to a couple key team members, but most were relieved.

I shared with everyone my philosophy that nonprofits cannot afford a lot of perks and benefits like their for-profit brethren, but what we can afford is flexibility and a culture that rewards work well done, not long hours. Beginning immediately, the most important tasks were doing the job well, treating each other with respect, and taking all of your vacation time so that you did not burn out and quit.

It was quite a paradigm shift for our little organization, and truthfully, for me as well. They did not know that I, too, was making a radical departure of my usual work ethic and hours. I had committed to no more midnight emails and no more manufactured urgency in this new role. I was going to create the kind of culture that I wanted to attract others to work in and we did this over the next few years.

Another amazing first for that year was that I went home to Michigan for Thanksgiving and we went skiing for Christmas. Since graduating from college, during every holiday I had been working in retail. I had *never*—and that is not an exaggeration—taken a Thanksgiving or a Christmas holiday off. Worse than that, I have spent Christmas Eve services refreshing my phone while reading West Coast numbers by candlelight trying to listen to my rector's homily.

THE CDA'S FIRST HARD YEAR (DITCH OF DESPAIR)

I have spent Christmas Day calling customers to apologize for ruining their holiday because a carrier overloaded their planes and left our hams (the customer's ham) on the runway in Kentucky or Memphis.

When I walked out of the door of the CDA to head home to see extended family on the Friday before Thanksgiving in 2016, I felt a freedom that was previously unknown to me. I savored it, texting my board an appreciation note that they were probably not expecting. Likewise, at Christmas, when we were able to take a trip to Park City, Utah, as a family, it was an amazing luxury of time.

A HANDS-ON WELCOME

Another incredible safety net for my first year was my board of directors, and especially my board chair Doug Higgins. Doug was on the search team that hired me and served for the first six months of my tenure. Doug is a bank president but has served on the CDA board since 2008. Some organizations have mandatory tenure limits. The CDA does not and for this I am grateful. Some of our most valuable and active board members would have been forced to roll off if we mandated limits on board service, including Doug.

Doug and I would meet regularly, at least monthly for breakfast and speak weekly on the phone. One of the questions that he often asked was whether I was in the "ditch of despair." This was a term that was shorthand for having a bad time of it, and not being in a good place mentally. Usually I was not exactly loving life on the job just yet, but not quite in the actual gully. But sometimes if I was in the ditch of despair, it was usually related to the building or something tied to facilities. There were many volunteer projects already underway and no weekend facilities person who was an appropriate representative to greet and supervise groups of volunteers. I didn't want to ask anyone to do anything that I wasn't willing and actively doing, so I dove in and led groups from companies, churches, and civic organizations, who came to beautify the playground and deep clean the classrooms.

I often found myself wondering what I had signed up for as I carried around five-gallon, orange Home Depot buckets filled with bleach water to give to volunteers in the classrooms as the water splashed onto my expensive pants. (Pro tip, don't wear expensive pants to supervise volunteer projects). I once suggested to the entire team that we rotate Saturdays and take turns with the volunteers, and then, instead, we'd get a day off during the week once every six weeks. This was met with a deafening silence as I asked them to consider a new way of operating. So instead, I found myself doing a lot of volunteer projects initially and wondering what I had done to my previously amazing career which now felt eerily similar to those Macy's stock room days.

I also found myself doing things that I never thought I would be doing, like sourcing parts for a thirty-year-old boiler and chiller that served as the heating and cooling for the entire school. It turns out that the iron pipes that ran water through the school as part of the system were disintegrating from the inside out. We would either need to replumb the entire school before replacing the boiler and the chiller, or invest in state-of-the-art Variant Refrigerant Flow (VRF) heating and cooling to the tune of an initial $800,000 estimate for the system. Welcome to the CDA!

In the interim, I needed to keep the current boiler running in the winter, which involved finding a replicator for our boiler. I didn't know what a replicator was, but I knew we needed one so I began to call around. My first call was to the facilities director at HoneyBaked, a highly skilled and experienced professional who nearly hung up when I called. He didn't believe it was actually me calling to ask about sourcing a part for a boiler. When he finished chuckling about how ironic it was that I was calling to ask about a part for a boiler when I wouldn't have even known we had heating and air units at HoneyBaked—because I had people to handle that—he helped me find a vendor out of Texas and I called and had the part overnighted.

The part came, the company came to fix it, but eventually, we had to raise money to put in a new VRF system and do some serious improvements in the school, including in maintenance personnel. All the while, Tommy proved to be a challenge to manage, with the work ethic of a sloth and about as sharp as a marble. Tommy, a licensed plumber, would still call a plumber in to fix a toilet or repair a leaking pipe, which was a waste of time and money. Tommy could still regularly be found sleeping in the outdoor screened classroom on the far end of our beautiful two-acre campus, perhaps sleeping off a joint that he had just finished based upon the odors that surrounded him. This was assuming that he showed up to work at all.

Finally, following several warnings and after consulting our board attorneys, we agreed that it was time for Tommy to be let go. I have an extensive background in Human Resources and have had termination discussions with hundreds of people in my career, yet it had been years since I had an exit conversation with anyone below the director level. So I was startled and a little offended when Tommy greeted my sensitively phrased pronouncement that he was

THE CDA'S FIRST HARD YEAR (DITCH OF DESPAIR)

being let go, after several previous performance discussions, with a loud and vigorous, "This is BULLSHIT, Miss Maggie!" Somehow putting "Miss" in front of my name didn't really soften the appalling affront to my sensibilities. I quickly told Tommy that the decision was final and that he needed to gather his things and leave the building as I escorted him out the door to my office. I returned to my office, closed the door and wondered, again, whether my whole career had gone up in smoke.

At our next board meeting, I ended the meeting with my usual "just one thing" which was a high-priority request that the board could rally around, above all others to help our mission (and me). This time my "just one thing" was help finding a high quality facilities person. Grace Shickler, our Chair-Elect, rose to the occasion in the biggest of ways. She called me after the meeting and said that she might have somebody. Boy, did she!

I've hired so many talented and amazing people in my thirty-year career, but none of them have made as much of a difference in my own quality of life as Chris Koke did when he agreed to take on the role of Facilities Director at the CDA. Chris is a real estate investor, a general contractor, and a man of great faith. He's also MacGyver-like in his ability to fix anything in the building without needing a contractor. (For those of you under forty, MacGyver was a popular TV character who could rig and configure anything out of whatever he had on hand.) Chris has put wheels on gates, installed foam playground flooring after learning from YouTube videos, and literally saved us hundreds of thousands of dollars while cheerfully saying "no problem" to nearly every request.

We try to be flexible with Chris's schedule as he is truly a renaissance man with a wide array of business and personal commitments, but he is also johnny-on-the-spot with us in an emergency.

Chris and his wife Maria are also foster parents and the CDA has been blessed to serve as the preschool for three of their foster daughters. Through Chris we have been blessed beyond measure and there aren't words enough to tell him what he has meant to the CDA during his tenure. Chris alone kept me from living in the ditch of despair during the latter part of the first year and allowed the CDA to do some really fun things.

One of the things that I wanted to do early in my tenure was rebrand the CDA. We were initially the North Fulton Child Development Association then the Child Development Association, which everyone abbreviated to the CDA. Those who knew of the CDA held it in very high esteem,

THE CDA'S FIRST HARD YEAR (DITCH OF DESPAIR)

and "CDA" had a lot of very positive brand equity and a very strong community reputation. While we did not want to lose that, too few people knew that we existed or what exactly we did. Many people confused us with the accrediting organization for Child Development Accreditation or the Center for Disease Control which is located in Atlanta.

Serendipity interceded in a beautiful way to solve two problems. In the fall of my first year, our literacy coach Yehymmy Mora innocently asked me how the toy drive for the Santa Shop was coming along. I asked her who was usually responsible for this and she said that the executive director was—that would be me. Glad I asked.

Again, I immediately started calling friends, neighbors, churches, and everyone that I could think of to start a toy drive as I was already behind. One of the calls that I made was to Steve and Kristin Harding, who were friends from our children's previous elementary school days at Roswell North Elementary (RNE). They had started a ministry called Bears Cares at RNE making sure that those children from families of lesser means had things that they needed, whether it was school supplies, a mattress to prevent them from sleeping on the floor, or jackets in the winter.

Steve and Kristin quickly put together a toy drive for us in their huge neighborhood, came for a tour, and were quickly regular volunteers. Then Steve joined our board. Steve was a partner in the ASO advertising firm and volunteered to lead a rebranding project for us at the CDA. He and his partner, Ryan Mikesell, worked with our Marketing Director Trish O'Neill to lead a full-fledged rebranding effort, ranging from internal interviews, board interviews, and a brand audit. They presented multiple concept options to the board and a new name and logo were accepted. ASO provided pro bono work to the tune of over a quarter of a million dollars of intellectual property and branding work to the CDA. Thank you again.

SMALL MUST BE STRATEGIC

Additionally, our internal team did a retreat offsite at my lake house in January of 2018 and presented a proposal to the board at our board strategic retreat in February 2018 for a new Mission, Vision and Values, which the board tweaked and adopted. Within the first two years, with the help of our team and an amazingly positive and supportive board, we had rebranded and drafted a new strategic plan, supported by a new mission, vision, and values.

One lesson that I learned in the first year, that has been drilled into me each subsequent year, is the importance of being truly strategic as a nonprofit leader. Strategy is as much about what you say no to doing as what you agree to do. With a board of over twenty highly engaged, creative, passionate and caring leaders, it is easy to become swept up in the latest great idea or enamored by what you see a competitor doing. Yes, other charities are actually competing for donor dollars. However, I've learned and been supported when I insist that we stick with our strategic priorities and table other really good ideas that require limited resources.

I, too, am sometimes guilty of coming up with a wild idea but we've instilled enough discipline among the team that even I am held in check from introducing ad hoc projects and non-strategically aligned priorities. We have even introduced a guideline that avoids starting sentences with "we should," instead preferring that an exciting, new initiative begins with "I would be willing to." It's amazing how much this limits the introduction of new initiatives.

There were some other memorable moments during Year One. Key among them is meeting the unforgettable Cy Mallard. Cy was the Pastor Emeritus of Roswell Presbyterian Church. He had been the active pastor during the founding years of the CDA and played a pivotal role at a time of great transition. The school had been meeting in volunteers' homes after its founding in 1967. The teachers were volunteers and the food was also provided by volunteers but the need was too great for a home-based program, so a fundraising campaign began to build a school on land that was being donated by the Grove Way Community Group.

In the interim, the founders had the idea to ask local churches if they might use their empty classrooms during the week to hold classes for the children. The story has it that the volunteers became very discouraged as church after church politely declined their request. While none of the churches were quite so honest, most presumed the fact that most students were Black was the primary reason for these churches turning down the request. Martin Luther King, Jr., famously said that "11 a.m. on Sunday is one of the most segregated hours, if not the most segregated hour, in Christian America." That was certainly true based upon the response received by the original CDA volunteer leaders, until they called Pastor Cy Mallard.

When Cy answered the phone, as told directly to me, he thought about it for a moment and told the caller, "Ladies, I'll deal with the Session." The Session is the lay leadership committee for the Presbyterian church. He continued with his precious Southern drawl. "But I'm going to assume that they've read Luke 18, Let the children come to me." And according to Cy, that was that.

THE CDA'S FIRST HARD YEAR (DITCH OF DESPAIR)

It was shocking to me as a Midwestern transplant to Atlanta to learn that my beloved Roswell still had segregated parks in the 1970s, as well as pastors who were not brave enough to allow Black children to attend preschool in their Sunday school rooms. Not to mention that people were so angry about the work of the CDA that a cross was burned on the corner of Grove Way and Bush Street *twice*, reportedly by the Ku Klux Klan, in protest of the education of young, Black children.

I became friends with Cy and his wife, Ann, visiting him at Roswell Presbyterian, in his home and becoming quite fond of him. I could write an entire book of Cy stories. He passed away in 2017, and it was a blessing to me that our paths crossed before he left this earth. The CDA has a field now named in his honor; Mallard Field. The sod was donated by Roswell Presbyterian Church and provides a grassy field for children who live predominantly in apartments to run and play. I know he would be pleased. I am so blessed to have been at the CDA in time to know him.

THANK GOD FOR GENEROUS FUNDERS

Another key first-year memory goes back again to North Point. While still in Year One, it came time to present our funding requests to North Point Community Church as part of their upcoming Be Rich campaign. Ameera Jo and her team sent me the Google Doc to complete with information about each project. Ameera was so patient with me when I filled out the document remotely and then naively called her to ask her how to save a Google Doc because I really just could not figure it out. Now, there may still be a few people in the world out there, like I was at the time, who are not aware that Google Docs update *automatically* so I was asking a very stupid question. Ameera didn't laugh at me and was very cognizant of the fact that I used to have two full-time administrative assistants within fifteen feet of my desk.

Ameera also was kind and patient when I went to meet with her and pastor Bryan Apinis, a pastor at North Point regarding our funding requests. I had left the financial request columns blank. When Ameera asked why I had left those columns blank, I told her quite frankly that I was uncomfortable asking for the money without a conversation first. One of the reasons that I credit her with a great deal of my success over the last seven years is that she has always coached me and supported me kindly. She gently but firmly told me that it was my job to be bold and think big. Instructively, she once told me that only when she told me to stop asking would I have asked for enough.

THE CDA'S FIRST HARD YEAR (DITCH OF DESPAIR)

Ameera's coaching paid off. I'm proud to say that in 2024, seven years later, she finally told me that we had asked for enough! Thank you, Ameera, Jadee, Pastor Bryan, Pastor Andy Stanley and every member of North Point Community Church who supports Be Rich. You have made such a difference, not just in my first year but every day at the CDA and with every child, along with so many other worthy causes across the globe. I personally think you are a generosity model for funders to study and follow.

I was also very fortunate in my first year, and blessed by a very large gift that was in the works as I joined the CDA. It was announced that Bob Hagan, his son Chad and daughter Brooke, through their family foundation, were donating a five-year, $150,000 challenge grant to the CDA to spur individual giving beginning in the fall of 2016. Each year, the Hagan Family Foundation would match $30,000 in individual giving for five years. It was one of the largest gifts from a private family in the history of the CDA. It was a very big deal. It generated a lot of buzz and gave our end-of-year Giving Tuesday campaign, and our entire fall an energy and excitement that would be impossible to match without it. It made a huge impact on that first year, and for the next five and beyond.

I would wish a Bob Hagan for every nonprofit. Not only

does he serve on our board, he also serves as a trusted advisor to me. I can literally pick up the phone and tell him any problem that is on my desk and he has wise advice or he will go to work helping me take care of it. If ticket sales for an upcoming event are slow, he will send out an email to friends and sell them. His business acumen and big heart make him a much sought-after board member, and we've been lucky to keep him on our board for my entire tenure. His entire family is a gift to our community. I cannot imagine my first years without his generosity and counsel.

Part of Bob's counsel, upon which we didn't see eye to eye, was whether or not I needed to join the local Rotary. My predecessor had been very involved in our local Rotary as was her husband. Besides Bob, I had several other Rotarians on my board and still do. Rose Burton, who ran HomeStretch, the nonprofit next door to us, was also an active member of the Rotary.

I am a *big fan* of Rotary International and the four very active Rotary Chapters that support the CDA regularly. Rotary does a lot of outstanding work around the world, including eradicating polio, once and for all. They also do a lot of excellent work in the local community. Rotarians, Kiwanians, Lions, Masons, Junior Leagues, Charity Guilds, NCL, YMSL and all of the various civic organizations that

THE CDA'S FIRST HARD YEAR (DITCH OF DESPAIR)

exist and support the nonprofits of the world are an extension of the work that we nonprofits do. Because of that, I have so much respect, admiration and deep appreciation for them.

I have so much admiration for what they do to support us, that it seemed redundant for me to join another nonprofit organization to which I would need to pay dues of a couple thousand dollars a year and require several hours during the week when we already had several Rotarian board members "representing us" as ambassadors. I wish I had the time to join every organization that volunteers and writes us a check. I wish I could personally let every single organization, big and small, know how much they mean to every organization they support. We could not do it without them. End of Sermon.

In my first year, my board was one of the greatest gifts that I was given. Doug Higgins, my board chair, was my rock and my constant cheerleader, coach and strategist. A bank president by day and a mentor extraordinaire in his extracurricular role, he reminds me so much of Chuck Bengochea, my corporate boss and mentor at HoneyBaked Ham. With Doug, like Chuck, you really had to listen for his coachings. Both men are elegant and full of class. Both men are Godly and wise, giving of themselves to invest in others and to make their communities better. There were also several members who were ready to roll off that stayed to give me an extra year of stability like Ron Hancock, a retired General Electric Executive who was an HR advisor to Jack Welch, and Richard Matherly, a local real estate investor who with his wife Susan are beloved advisors, just to name a few. Brock Darby was a wonderful asset until he was moved to my motherland, Michigan, with Home Depot. I still miss that board member.

In my first year, I learned that one of our annual events was a caroling event that involved board members and friends dressing up in Santa costumes and collecting money in local restaurants in December, while consuming a good bit of Christmas cheer representing the CDA. Apparently there was some franchise licensing discrepancy with this event as well as a bit of a concern about the appropriateness of a preschool board drinking and caroling through the streets of Roswell. I unilaterally made the decision to cancel after trying to negotiate the franchise licensing deal. Acting as if I were the CEO of a private entity, I failed to consult anyone. Oops.

Doug reached out and oh so graciously advised me that while he agreed with the decision and why I had made it, in the future it might be a better idea to reach out to the execu-

THE CDA'S FIRST HARD YEAR (DITCH OF DESPAIR)

tive committee in advance and advise them before announcing it to the entire board. I fully understood his position and totally agreed. I had blown it. But Doug didn't make me feel like I had made a fatal error. He has a gift for correction that is subtle and personal. I am sure he is wonderful to work for in a full-time capacity.

Our board has an unusual practice in that we elect a new board chair every year. It seems like just as a new board chair and I are hitting our stride, it is time to introduce a new board chair. As I met with Virginia Hepner with the Woodruff Arts Center, she advised me against going to work for an organization that had a new board chair every year. However, I have to say that I haven't found it untenable. One of my board chairs, Catherine Storey, agreed to stay and serve two terms due to Covid. Thank you, Cat. By and large, it is manageable. I am the one that needs to adapt. It enables us to attract really talented individuals because we are only asking for a few years of commitment to the executive committee rotation.

In May of my first year, I got to experience the first of what is often a necessary evil for nonprofits—the fundraising event. At the time, our biggest fundraiser, which netted about $50,000 for the school, was The Down Home Derby. It was the brainchild of my predecessor and a local event planner. While well attended, it was a beast to put on. The CDA literally took a local horse farm and turned it into a party venue for one night, renting nearly everything.

After attending the event and returning home, I literally cried while talking to my husband Bob about it. I felt like only half of the people attending even knew what cause they were supporting that night. The event felt very disconnected from our mission. Our team, especially Trish O'Neill, our previous Marketing Director, and Chris Koke, worked incredibly hard to put on the event, and the juice seemed barely worth the squeeze.

The following Monday when we debriefed the event, we captured what we liked about the event and what we wished were different. At the next board meeting, I made a presentation to the board discussing the potential of ditching the Derby in lieu of something else. That idea was met with a unanimous thud. They wanted me to fix the economics of the event and improve the mission communications of the event, but the CDA owned Derby Saturday in our community and we were not going to give that up. Message heard.

Through the hard work of Chris Koke and Trish O'Neill and then Trish's successor and eventually my successor as Executive Director at the CDA; Sheila Sillitto, the Derby is now a very profitable event and much easier to host as Shei-

THE CDA'S FIRST HARD YEAR (DITCH OF DESPAIR)

la found a horse farm party venue. I'm now a big fan of the Down Home Derby and look forward to it thanks to the generosity of our donors and those that love it. It now regularly nets over $100,000 and is worth the effort, plus I love the chance to wear the big hats when we are actually making money and telling people about our kids.

I'm an even bigger fan of an event that we have added that we hold in the fall at our own facility, Party On Our Playground. It is affectionately known to insiders by its acronym. I'll give you a minute to think about it...

Created in the wake of COVID and a desire to have an outdoor event, Sheila Sillitto whipped up this event in a matter of months, a description belying the amount of work that went into it, but one of the many reasons that Sheila has taken over my role as leader of the CDA. My friends Tom and Dana Moore did the amazing party graphic logo. It is now a staple on our calendar and I love inviting the community to come and see our precious school and walk around our playground with a glass of wine under the twinkle lights that volunteers install for us.

Who would have thought, as I slopped buckets around the playground in that first year, that we would have come so far as to have an elegant soiree on that same playground now? If I'm honest with myself, in those initial months I had doubts whether I'd still be there at the end of Year One, but only slight doubts.

A HIGHLY DESIRED WORKPLACE

After twenty-plus years operating at the very strategic and non-tactical level, it was a shock to my system to not just be responsible for tactical details, but to actually be performing manual labor. It was, again, humbling. But it was also empowering to know that I can clean a playground building or get chewing gum off the bottom of a cafeteria table as well as the next person. I am not too precious to roll up my sleeves and pitch in. The first year showed me that I could do (most of) those hard things, but also prompted me to figure out solutions on how to get out of doing those things regularly, because it is not my highest and best use.

I would say, in hindsight, that I am most proud of the culture that we have created at the CDA. We have created a flexible, best-in-class workplace where our teachers and staff want to work and where retention is high. We close the school between Christmas and New Year's, when enrollment is low, to give teachers an extra paid week off.

The nonprofit sector is known for burning out their often underpaid work force, but that does not have to be the case.

We can hire talented individuals and give them something that others can't; flexibility within a purpose-driven career that makes a difference in the world. That is something the next generation of workers crave.

Actually, it is what everyone craves.

CHAPTER 7

SEE CHANGES

THE world immediately sees you differently the minute you evolve from holding a big job at one of America's most beloved brands to being the CEO or Executive Director at a small, local nonprofit—no matter how noble and essential the mission. People were universally supportive and positive about my new role, but almost all in a quasi-sympathetic fashion. I am not sure that anyone but my closest friends and family believed that I really chose this path, much less chased it and wrestled it to the ground.

I have a dear friend and mentor, who was one of the most supportive and gracious advocates for me and the CDA from the very beginning of my tenure. Randy Hain is an author, consultant and coach who also serves on several nonprofit boards. He held an entire symposium to highlight me as a speaker to the local business community on the importance of high-quality early education and some of my dearest friends showed up, as well as some friends that I hadn't seen in years. Randy also spoke at several of my board retreats and he never came to the CDA without dropping off a *very* generous check. Over the holidays during my first year at the CDA, he encouraged his clients and friends who might be looking to send him a Christmas gift to donate to the CDA in his honor, instead. Wow!

I am embarrassed to say that when Randy tried to call on me when I was in HR for business development with HoneyBaked, I was not as gracious with my time. Not even close.

AN INDELIBLE FREE LUNCH

However, one of the lasting memories of my initial time with Randy after I joined the CDA was when we were having lunch at our favorite meeting site, Thai House on Crossville Road in Roswell. I can't remember what Randy ordered, but I ordered the cashew chicken. Randy and I would go to lunch every few months or so without fail. On one of the occasions I attempted to put my American Express card out before he could pay, but he quickly rebuffed the effort. I can't remember my earnest attempt to pay, but I do remember his rebuttal to the effect of "Yes, but one of us runs a nonprofit." End of discussion.

I know to the core of my being that it was not intended as anything other than a sincere attempt to allow him to get the check and probably expense it through his business, but it was reflective of how it saw me now. Less able to pay.

Randy didn't know that I worked at Circuit City when it was one of *Forbes*' top performing stocks, and I had both grants and options. Randy didn't know that my previous CEO at HoneyBaked had put a deferred compensation plan into existence that was supplementing my experiment into voluntary socialism and good works. He just knew that his billable hourly rate was probably ten times my hourly rate. He was not wrong, and he is *very* generous.

Most everyone, however, assumed that we were poor now, including my children who had no idea how much we had saved for this experiment. They didn't know what it meant when they asked if we were rich and I always said no but we were comfortable.

WHO MOVED MY CHEESE?

I have to say that the biggest sea change happened at home. My boys were used to a nanny who had moved into a household manager when they went to school. Her job now was to make my life, Bob's life, and their lives easier as I traveled and worked what I used to call the "big job". We called Stephanie Stephenson the "wife that Bob and I both deserved". She was so much more than that. She was my dearest friend, my confidant, my sister and the boys' surrogate mother. At one point, she was my children's designated guardian were anything to happen to Bob and myself, so entrenched was she in our family. When I came home in May 2016 with my lone copy box of personal effects, Stephanie knew that our ten-year run was over. Even though she regularly had summers off as my husband was a teacher and coach who had eight weeks off in the summer, it was the end of an era for us all.

I started packing the kids' lunches immediately in May and soon received a text message from my oldest son, who informed me that I had not put American cheese on his sandwich. I texted back my sincere apologies, telling him that I was on the way to the school post haste. I would have Mr. Huff, the high school principal who was also a dear friend, use the school intercom to notify him and the student body immediately that his mommy was in the office with his piece of American cheese as soon as I got there.

He replied, "You are kidding, right?" I was joking but I was happy that he was just a little uncertain. Later that night we had a discussion about his text when he replied, with a perfectly serious face, that "I am just trying to help you learn the way I like things. Mrs. Stephenson already knew." I realize then just how entitled my children's lives were. They were more than comfortable — they were spoiled.

A few weeks later, I was searching for something and had occasion to go upstairs in one of the boys' rooms and was shocked by what I found in both of their rooms. The chaos was reminiscent of the Dust Bowl of the 1930s. There were clothes everywhere. Since Bob and my bedroom was on the main floor and Stephanie had always done the boys' laundry, made their beds, and the cleaning lady had regularly cleaned up their rooms, I had little reason to ever venture upstairs. In fact, it occurred to me that I could not remember the last time that I had been upstairs.

Life was really changing for me at the day-to-day level even before I landed the new gig. I was a little spoiled too.

My husband Bob is very frugal. I originally described him as a miser, but he asked me to edit that out when he read the draft of this book. This was my compromise. Bob did not grow up with a lot of extra spending money and even beyond this, he loves to exaggerate their level of "poverty" to our two sons. The truth is that they were solidly middle class but he likes to tell stories to the boys that make them sound dirt poor. We have occasionally taken to getting his mom, Grandma Donna, on the phone to verify his stories of destitution. She usually rats him out for embellishing, but occasionally she will say, "No, that is true, he did get underwear for Christmas and no, we did not have a dishwasher or a snowblower until after he went to college."

Between the two of us, we eventually had to come to an understanding that I had a "big job" with a "big paycheck" and he didn't get to question every purchase that I made. The day of reckoning happened over asparagus. We were in the car on a trip and were talking about dinner the evening before where we had chicken and asparagus on the grill. I had actually done the grocery shopping, which was a rarity, so he randomly asked me how much the asparagus had cost. I glibly answered that I did not know.

He was incredulous. He asked for a ballpark amount. I quipped back at him that it was likely less than $100 a stalk. He fumed. I said, "I wanted asparagus so I bought asparagus. What's the big deal? I'm pretty sure that if it rang up at more than $100 per stalk I would have noticed, but otherwise, not a clue." He literally could not imagine that I did not have any estimate of how much last night's side vegetable cost.

I think he began to shake, and I definitely saw a vein pop out of his forehead as he started to rant when I stopped him and with a raised voice said, "Give me a number. Tell me what I need to make for you to stop asking me about what asparagus costs and other nonsensical things and I will make it." There might have been a profanity tossed in there, but the boys were in the back seat so maybe not. He stared at me for a millisecond before turning back to the road and wisely replied, "I think you already do." Going forward, whenever a fight over money was about to start, asparagus became my safe word.

It was a bellwether moment in our marriage. I am a "life is short" and impulsively generous person that is married to a frugal partner but he had to adjust back then. Now, even though we had considerable savings, most of it was in tax-preferred retirement funds, so I was going to do some adjustment based strictly on monthly cash flow. Things were definitely changing. I was going to have to learn the price of asparagus.

Humbled on Purpose

FROM GIVER TO ASKER

I have seldom been turned down when I have asked someone to do something for the CDA, or me. It is why it is easy to stay in a perpetual state of gratitude, and I don't think that it is as tiring to me as it seems. When I started at the CDA, I asked the outgoing CDA what constituted a "major gift." The answer was $100. I was shocked but the data backed up her answer, there were very few donors that gave more than $100 annually who did not serve on the board. We had a lot of work to do.

Thanks to The Hagan Family Challenge, and a lot of work cultivating individual giving, in 2023 we rolled out "Giving Circles" which are recognition levels that provide extra perks to those that give over $1,000 (Believers), $2,500 (Sustainers), and $5,000 (Champions). I am proud to say that we have well over 100 households now that are annual members of our Giving Circles.

We also have a monthly recognition program for those that give at least $25 a month that we call the Mallard Flock, a lovely tribute to Cy Mallard and his wife Ann and all that they have meant to the CDA.

I also began to be very conscious of my trappings of wealth or the way I would see myself. My big splurge for my fiftieth birthday, while still working for HoneyBaked, had been a large Louis Vuitton handbag. The cost of this satchel-sized bag, which was a rare purchase for me, would now pay for too many days of preschool for a child for me to admit. Suddenly, it made me feel ostentatious. However, at the same time, I was also calling on donors for whom I did not need to dress down, so there was a constant struggle between being true to who I was and avoiding appearing to be someone that I was not when I walked in the door. I drove a little Acura SUV that did not stand out too much, but at the same time I was glad that I no longer drove the Mercedes sedan.

I did begin to notice that there were many executive directors that had even nicer clothes, jewels, handbags and cars than I did. A lot of executive directors were women whose husbands were the major breadwinners in the house and they had worked their way up from social worker or even volunteer to run these organizations. I'm not sure if they had qualms about their outward trappings of wealth. That said, even if so, they seemed to adapt or get over them as they made no attempt to dumb down what they were wearing, driving or carrying.

I'm not saying I saw myself as some sort of savior of small children, but I did consciously think about what I spent on our lake house, our club membership, and our bigger-than-needed first home. Several times a year, I would come into the office and find a person experiencing homelessness sleeping in front of the entrance to our office with their phone plugged into our outside electrical plug and their back to the wall for security, warmth and wind protection. That same evening, I would drive a mile northwest to my seemingly palatial six-bedroom home and wonder what Jesus would do with the house's three empty bedrooms.

That's not true. I didn't really wonder. I know in my heart that Jesus would have brought the homeless home. While I could feel a sea change in my heart, I never brought the homeless back to our house with me, but I did feel my heart changing, and it made it more challenging to live in one world and work in another day by day. I didn't bring the homeless into my home with two teenagers, but it did cause me to revisit my previous political beliefs and embrace something that I refer to as voluntary socialism.

FROM EACH, ACCORDING TO THEIR MEANS

Previously, I had been a fairly staunch economic conservative. I believed in George W. Bush's label of "compassionate conservatism" and was an admirer of his father's vision of private nonprofits blanketing the nation with thousands of points of light and goodness serving as a safety blanket for the poor and the needy. I have come to personally believe that we need far greater voluntary socialism, from each according to their means and to each according to their needs. And, at the risk of giving up my Libertarian party card, I think we should pay higher taxes to provide a greater safety net to our citizens.

I have come to believe that universal health care is a human right and should be a global right, not just in the United States. This extends to mental health care as well, the brain is a bodily organ— how did the insurance companies and their lobbyists ever get this separated out? I think that everyone on the globe should have food to eat and clean water to drink—who doesn't? I think that everyone should have a roof over their head and a job to do that brings in a living wage. There are enough resources in the world for this to happen, they are just not distributed correctly.

Don't get me started on the fact that all children should have access to high-quality early education. I was once on the phone with a private equity partner, giving a reference on a former colleague and we ventured off on to the topic of childcare after he had perused my LinkedIn profile. They had recently nearly made an acquisition of a franchise early education chain, but stopped short based on the challenging economics of childcare with cost to parents being at a breaking point and teacher pay still needing to rise. He challenged me with an interesting proposition. He asked if I were the Early Education Czar of the United States how would I solve the problem, and he kept pushing until I gave him my vision. I'm glad he did, because when we hosted a round table with U.S. Senator Jon Ossoff, I was able to share this with him and he didn't disagree.

I told the venture capitalist and Senator Ossoff that I strongly believe that parents should have more paid leave to be home with their babies for longer than six weeks, even up to a year split between two parents. There should be more subsidies to provide quality childcare for infants to toddlers up to two years old. I believe that public education should start at age three and continue until everyone has a trade or is enrolled in an appropriate community college or university more like is done in Europe and Asia.

Whose pie in the sky ideas are these? The truth is that there is plenty of money to enact this craziness, but it is sitting in the hands of private citizens and corporations. We can either get more aggressive about voluntary socialism or there is going to be a day of reckoning where real socialism may find its way to us as the impoverished rise up to demand their share of the world's wealth. I personally believe that people are generous by nature and we just need to encourage the behavior more, rather than eliminating the incentive as we have been doing with our tax reform recently.

Too many people get their political direction and voting booth guidance from strangers on the television, radio and Internet rather than really contemplating the kind of world that they want to live in and supporting candidates accordingly. There is certainly no one party, and definitely no single candidate, that represents everything that I believe across every issue or funding need. However, I do know the kind of country that I do not want to live in. I do not want to be part of a society that does not support its children and I am going to vote that way every opportunity that I have. That's just one more positive change that came from being humbled on purpose.

Nobody needs as much money as Jeff Bezos or Elon Musk. Should we wait until the billionaires pass away for their vast wealth to be redistributed, per their pledge, into the mainstream of society and allow them to decide where it goes? Why do the Vatican and the great monarchies of the world need to own such a large percentage of the world's assets when such a large percentage of the world goes to bed each night, including children, without clean water or full bellies? These questions did not trouble me eight years ago but they do now. Deeply.

The way that the world sees me now has definitely changed. I am not the privileged and special executive that once merited special treatment, free tickets and reserved parking spots. Nor am I the hardened conservative who once believed that many of the poor are poor because of their choices and if they just worked a bit harder, they too could live like the rest of us. I know better now and I can't unlearn what I have learned.

One of my deepest regrets with taking an 86 percent pay cut to take this job is that I have less disposable income with which to be generous to those in need. However, I am still operating in an income bracket that most families at the CDA will never know and I do not forget that. In fact, I now give a larger percentage to charity than I did when I was making far more. Strange how that happens ...

One of my mementos, of which I am most proud, is from my time in Ann Arbor. Yep, I'm using a go back card again. It is a round maize and blue "M Go Fritz" pin (Fritz was Walter Mondale's nickname) from the Reagan vs. Mondale election of 1984 that I proudly wore on my Guess jean jacket. Even in his historic loss, Mondale carried Ann Arbor and the state of Minnesota. I was a political science major and campaigned for Mondale. My sons can't believe that I missed the opportunity to vote for the greatest president ever, in their opinion, Ronald Reagan.

Bob says that I am now right back to where I was in the 1980s politically but I have evolved. However, one thing is certain—I am a product of my experiences and have been shaped by all of them.

There is a saying that "If you aren't a liberal in your twenties you have no heart, but if you aren't a conservative by your fifties you have no brain." I used to believe that, but now I believe that there is another evolution as our basic needs are met and we become more self-actualized.

However, the world is so polarized now as Tik Tok and X feed us algorithms that influence us to be even more conservative or liberal, missing the chance, like I did, to experience the evolution from being a Mondale supporter to a George W. Bush compassionate conservative. Or the desire to take the world's shortest political quiz and discover that you're actually a Libertarian.

In my case, I'm often so disgusted by the extremes of both parties that I have transitioned to help causes I care about more directly. In 2024, I returned from a mission trip to Honduras and my views evolved further. Wouldn't money earmarked to build a wall be better spent building schools in Latin America and helping those countries fight their crippling unemployment? I would love for a moderate to lead us out of this polarized mess, but this seems like a pipe dream in our extremely polarized climate. Anyone?

OUR CALL TO GIVE BACK

Pastor Andy Stanley, founder of North Point Ministries, in his book, *How to Be Rich*, says "It's not how much you have, it's what you do with what you have." I have definitely found that to ring true time and time again. There are many people who are so generous with their limited means and others who give largely, but I really don't know if it is sacrificial or not. Some love to give publicly, and some give lavishly but in secret. I tend to have to give publicly so that others can see me as a pace car for our organization, but I love those that like to secretly hand me a check.

There is a generous donor who gives anonymously to our Santa Shop each year. They once came for a tour of our school and heard me telling the story of our Santa Shop and how parents would line up early to make sure that their child could get a bike because we didn't get enough bikes donated each year. Bikes are expensive, even sixteen-inch bikes with training wheels. This donor was deeply struck by this story to the point that they called me immediately to follow up. They asked how many bikes we would need to ensure that each pre-K child received a bike, as well as the price. I told this donor that we would need sixty bikes and they cost about $100 each, but we usually received about thirty, so we would just need an additional thirty bikes.

The following week we received a check from their donor advised fund for $3,000. The story does not end there. The donor continues to ensure each year that we receive enough bikes for each pre-K child. They decline to be identified not because they don't want to be solicited by a lot of other charities—which would be a legitimate concern as it is a very competitive industry. However, in this case, they are generous from their heart and I think they know they will get their crowns in heaven. This year they also bought helmets to go with every bike. I wish I could shout thank you and their name to the top of the rafters, but I'll just say thank you and they will know they are appreciated. Thank you, good and kind neighbor.

People do not like children to suffer. They see them as blameless victims. Unfortunately they do not see adults in poverty the same way. They do not understand that many families across America are one medical crisis, one job loss, or one unexpected financial hardship away from near ruin. When I go to speak about the CDA with groups, I'm often asked whether our parents provide any "sweat equity" for their children's education. In other words, do they clean the school, do odd jobs, etc., in return for their free or nearly free tuition? My answer is usually a gentle education about the typical daily schedules of our families, and how they work very hard and sacrifice to even get their children to our school. They do not have extra time to clean the school or volunteer, although they would love to do those sorts of things. Volunteering is a very middle class activity.

There are so many false beliefs about the poor in our country. While I didn't believe in all of them, I didn't actively disbelieve them previously. Now I *know* that most people aren't poor because they are on drugs or made poor choices. It is hard to break out of generational poverty without a hand up.

That is what the CDA is all about: breaking the cycle of generational poverty. My office looks out over the playground and when I look out and see the children running across Mallard Field, I can visualize them growing into productive adults whose children will not need the CDA thus ending the cycle of poverty. That is lasting, generational change.

CHAPTER 8

WHY THE CDA?

HIGH-QUALITY early education was not at the top of my list of passion projects to follow into nonprofit work, far from it. It was not really on my radar at all. I had three distinct ideas and none of them involved adorable toddlers doling out knee hugs.

I was fairly certain that I wanted to make an impact in the areas of mental health, women in leadership, or food insecurity—which was a purpose that remained important to me from my days at HoneyBaked. All three areas of potential impact were personally connected to me and my life and I felt that I could really dig in with authenticity and zeal.

Then, after being told about the potential opening at the CDA, I learned more about the important work of Dr. James Heckman. Heckman won the Nobel Prize in economics in 2000 for something called the "Heckman Curve." His work shows that, in general, the highest return on social investment comes from the earliest investment in children, particularly, at-risk children from low-income households.

THE IMPACT OF INVESTING IN EARLY EDUCATION

In fact, for each dollar invested in children before the age of six, seven dollars will be returned. If you take that same dollar and invest it in high-risk children, those children who come from low-income households, you will receive thirteen dollars back for each dollar invested. Wow! This is a foundational impact. This is the work being done at the CDA, by Head Start and others.

Early education is also transformative in that it fixes future problems. If you provide high-quality early education to children from the ages of birth until five years old, they are more likely to be ready to learn in kindergarten, read on level by third grade, and graduate from high school. If they graduate from high school, they are more likely to attend college, have a better paying job, pay taxes, not end up incarcerated, and not have unplanned pregnancies. It is also a fact that they are more likely to have intact families, or not get divorced, which I still believe is a good thing.

It also seemed obvious to me that these things would also mean that they are far less likely to ever suffer from food insecurity. The girls that attend the CDA are more likely to see themselves as leaders earlier in their lives than those who do not have the benefit of high quality early education with a social-emotional curriculum.

Even mental-health issues are less likely to be prevalent in children who are deemed ready for kindergarten, and not labeled developmentally delayed or behavior challenged. At the CDA we have a social/emotional curriculum for our students. They are taught to use their words when they are angry. They are taught to breathe deeply when they feel like hitting. We teach them meditation and even do yoga with them. These early lessons are lasting and result in them being less likely to grow up to bully or even *be* bullied.

Additionally, children who have never had the opportunity to be asked to sit still for fifteen minutes, nap on a cot, or put their things in a cubby are not likely to be able to do it readily on the first day or even the first week of kindergarten, compared to their peers with early education experience. Plus children who know their colors, shapes, and letters when they enter kindergarten are thought to be smarter than peers who have not been to preschool where they learned those things.

While flawed, the number one predictor of a child's intelligence entering kindergarten is often their ability to read. Imagine how far behind a child who has spent their most formative years in home childcare with a neighbor watching several families' children economically compared with a child who attended a National Association for the Education of Young Children. The truth is that children without preschool might not have intelligence gaps. Instead, what actually exists is an opportunity gap.

If every child had access to high-quality early education, not just warehousing of young children, with low teacher-to-children ratios, excellent nutrition, loving care, open-ended questioning, and an interesting curriculum of play-based learning, American schools would be much further along. In high quality centers, children who need extra support would be diagnosed much earlier and resources provided when they can do the most good for the child and the family. If everyone had access to merely adequate early care, far more citizens would be able to go to work daily secure in the fact that their children were engaged in meaningful educational activities preparing them to begin school, ready to learn and excel in kindergarten. There is enough money to do this in the United States; it just needs to become a priority.

MY OWN EARLY EDUCATION

It was only after starting at the CDA that my own early childhood experience resonated with what I was learning about the importance of the first 5 years. I learned about the simple ten question quiz called the Adverse Childhood Experience (ACE) Quiz. It measures the amount of trauma that a child experiences and is predictive of physical and mental health challenges later in life. Most children from low-income or at-risk households face more challenges than their two-parent, middle-class peers.

Here is the link for those of you who would like to take it yourself.

https://americanspcc.org/take-the-aces-quiz

A score of four or more is considered to be significantly at risk. Imagine my surprise when uber successful, Maggie Michaels DeCan took the test and learned my score was an EIGHT. I was shocked but not really after reading the questions. While my worst trauma happened when I was too young to remember, research shows that trauma is stored in the body at the cellular level and thus is remembered. Whether I consciously recall it or not, my body does.

It's interesting to take your ACE quiz. I've done it with many groups of friends. We once did it on the way home from a weekend lady's tennis trip to the beach. Not only was I the high score, I was the only score higher than 1. We took it as an office team as an exercise, most of my teammates were zeros. If you study the quiz, the answers are all or nothing. Where I had to give myself a point was in very mild circumstances, in some cases, but I did have a lot of trauma and I also suffer some of the predictable health effects like migraines and depression.

However, I also had a secret weapon in my preschool years, my mom. My "new" mom was a godsend. My parents tried to send me to preschool, but my separation anxiety from losing Mary and then my nanny, Dorothy Brown, was profound. I was pronounced too emotionally immature to attend and sent home. My mom was very concerned that I would not be ready for kindergarten, much like those kind-hearted women in Roswell, she set about getting me ready to go to school.

Imagine my first teacher, Mrs. Van Osdol's, reaction when Maggie Michaels joined her class and could tell time and let her know when it was time for nap time to end. And I regularly did. I'm sure that Mrs. Van Osdol really appreciated my help reading aloud all the story books and even some of the chapter books. Colors, shapes and animals, those were easy for me. Numbers, did you want those forward or backwards? Did you want them by twos, fives or tens? Precocious is a word that is written often in beautiful cursive handwriting across my student reports from North Hill Elementary.

I also had a confidence that was interpreted for early signs of leadership that was noted on my early progress reports. Was it a manifestation of my desire to control the universe and my kindergarten class or the result that I was probably two grade levels ahead thanks to Carol's creative homeschooling and mission to make sure that I was ready. The schools talked to my parents about having me skip grades several times, but my parents never opted for that fearing that it would harm me emotionally, and they were probably right to not advance me.

I think back at how I was labeled 'intelligent' immediately upon entering the public school system because I could read and was so far ahead of my classmates. My Iowa Basic test scores quickly backed this up, again supported by years of individualized, focused attention by my mom. I went to

Humbled on Purpose

my own "CDA" (Carol's Development Academy) and it paid off early and often.

However, it wasn't all fun and games. One especially poignant memory involves my sixth birthday, or rather the day before my sixth birthday. Carol had dropped off beautifully decorated cupcakes at school for my birthday. Mrs. Van Osdol and her aid excitedly began to pass out the cupcakes when I announced that I was not participating today. When they asked me why, I told them it was not my birthday. They laughed and told me that it most certainly was and that I would sit down and let the class sing to me.

I continued to refuse. (I could be pretty stubborn when pushed, then and now.) The behavior escalated until they marched me in my little navy jumper and patent leather shoes with white ankle socks up to the principal's office to call my mom and report my atrocious and highly unusual behavior.

After calling my mom and reporting my awful behavior, she asked to put me on the phone. I can still hear the horror in her voice as she asked me when exactly I thought my birthday was. As I told her that my birthday was definitely January 11th, not today, it registered that she had gotten my birthday wrong by a single day. She apologized profusely and said that she would make it up to me.

WHY THE CDA?

I remember the mood of the teachers going from anger to horrified sympathy wondering what kind of mother mistakes their kindergartener's birthday? I did not want their sympathy and I stubbornly walked back down to the classroom as if nothing had happened.

I never let my mom off the hook on my birthday or helped her. I never reminded her. I never told her it was coming. In middle school she got confused and thought it was the 12th. My dad was traveling, so it passed with nothing to mark it until she started to make a cake on the 12th and I told her it was already over. When she asked why I didn't say anything, I told her that I just didn't.

The truth is my mom says that I raised myself. I made my own lunches beginning in kindergarten. I didn't want to bother anyone for anything, ever. That was part of earning my own place on earth. If you don't need anything from anyone, you will never be disappointed. It's a terrible way to go through life as a child or as an adult. It took a lot of therapy to get over my lessons learned in those early years and I would say that my husband, Bob, as a boyfriend, was the first person that I ever came to depend upon and now, forty-six years later, he's never really let me down. I often thought that unlike the unconditional love of the dogs or my sons who are growing up and will have their own amazing lives, it is Bob who God gifted to me to make up for some of my early losses.

As for my mom, Carol, in therapy, I learned that Carol, while not perfect, was a bit of a saint to marry my dad and take on his three kids at her age. I remember when I was 25 being very cognizant of just how young I was and not being able to imagine doing what she did for our family. Thanks again, Mom.

While my genetic intellect might come from my dad, my nurtured intellect and the great start that I got in school came from my mom. We would go to the library. She taught me to love reading. I would read biographies and Nancy Drew and anything that I could get my hands on. She was a homeschooler before there was homeschooling and she did it for my older brother when he was struggling as well. This is one road not traveled that I don't like to imagine. I can't imagine what my early years would have been like, what my kindergarten would have been like, without Carol's extra attention and help.

It's so rewarding now to pay it forward. I wonder if subconsciously this is why the CDA immediately caught my attention and drew me in, and made me fight for the opportunity. Next year the CDA, with funding help from the very generous Goizueta Foundation, is rolling out Home-Based

Learning for parents who cannot get their young children to the CDA. We are going to create an army of Carols and that is a *very* good thing.

PAYING TEACHERS WHAT THEY ARE WORTH

I want to live in a world where preschool teachers are our superheroes. We just gave raises to our teachers when we had trouble reopening some of our classrooms after COVID and competing with the fast food restaurants. So now, based upon education, tenure, and certifications, our lead teachers make up to $25 an hour and our assistant teachers make as much as $22 an hour. To our knowledge, we are one of the highest paying early education centers in the state of Georgia.

It immediately solved our staffing issue and we have nearly 100 percent retention. *It really is the money, stupid,* I said to myself after the solution was this simple. However, we are also raising the standards for what we expect of our education professionals in terms of punctuality, attendance, personal phone usage and other pet peeves that we used to tolerate when replacement was nearly impossible.

We *love* our teachers and try to show it with respect, compensation and a benefits package that meets their greatest needs so that they show that same love to their students.

Humbled on Purpose

When NAEYC and Georgia Quality Rated come to inspect, we hope they see the level of professionalism in our classrooms is as far above other schools as our compensation.

I certainly didn't set out to become a trendsetter for early education in the state of Georgia, but necessity is the mother of invention and as a team, we developed a solution that I hope others can follow. If our nonprofit center can figure it out charging $75 to $105 a week per child, surely for-profit centers charging $450 per child per week can figure out how to pay their best caregivers better salaries, too. Those who care for our most valuable resource deserve to be fairly compensated and we will also see more qualified professionals entering the industry and fewer cases of abuse and neglect as well.

Every child deserves a great start. From conception to graduation, we, as a society, really owe children, globally, the best that we can offer. While national security funding is important, right up there next to it should be early education and childcare.

I did not know this when I signed on, but I was signing up with a mission that should be the easiest sale in the world because we already have a Nobel Prize in economics backing our outcomes; The Heckman Equation. If donors want to make sure that their dollars will see a return in just one generation of 13 times their investment, donate to early education for at-risk children. Learn more at https://heckmanequation.org/.

CHAPTER 9

GOOD COMPANY(IES)

NOBODY should feel that they have to go into nonprofit work to find meaningful work or joy in their daily life.

My own journey was a progression. From the toxic existence of the sales floor at Macy's in the mid-80's, to the relative calm of the HR department and a more family friendly retailer in Belk, to a multi-unit HR environment surrounded by amazing mentors who looked out for my career and maximized my talent at Circuit City, I then finally journeyed to find HoneyBaked. Chuck's values-based leadership, first started by Dick Farbolin in the 1970's, made for an amazing *for*-profit workplace.

FINDING PURPOSE IN THE FOR-PROFIT WORLD

Even within the corporate world, now you can often join a company's community service committee and most companies have built-in volunteer opportunities, frequently within the work day. This generation entering the workforce is demanding that their employers do more than just provide jobs and dividends to stakeholders. They insist on working for organizations that give back to their communities in a meaningful way with time, talent and treasure.

If you are lucky enough to work for a company that has a cause-marketing initiative or a community-impact committee, offering to serve on it can be a tremendous opportunity to feed your soul at work. Often, these committees yield tremendous authority on which organizations get the company's support in terms of volunteer hours, grant dollars and other perks.

At the CDA we like to say that given just one person's name at a company, we can usually, within a year, find our way into the right circle to become an organization with which the company volunteers. If you do a good job with volunteers, something that the CDA prides ourselves on,

GOOD COMPANY (IES)

good things follow. These include checks, which can come in the way of sponsorships or grants. We love either or both.

Even if your existing company does not have a community outreach program, it does not mean that they couldn't start one or that *you* couldn't start one. Perhaps they just haven't had anyone raise their hand and volunteer to do so yet. When I was a still relatively young HR manager at Circuit City, our offices were located on the westside of Atlanta, off the Bankhead Highway connected to our distribution center.

Located next to us was the notorious Bankhead Courts, also known as Bankhead Homes. It was notorious for crime and gang activity that was reported regularly on the evening news. It wasn't overly hyped news as every now and again there were bullet casings in the parking lot and occasionally stray bullets found a windshield or the door of a car parked in our employee parking lot. Circuit City was intentionally located there as it was an Economic Opportunity Zone with tax credits designed for placing your business in a blighted economic area and hiring employees from the local community. The hope was that residents of Bankhead Homes could find employment at the Circuit City or other distribution centers that opened.

The experiment, however, did not work out as expected as Circuit City had a very rigorous application process that included drug screening and polygraph tests based upon the highly desirable and expensive products that ran through our distribution center. Very few local candidates were able to pass the screening. It's hard to take a twenty-year-old without structure, support or training and turn them into a polished job applicant. On the other hand, if you enroll that same child at the CDA as a preschooler, we can prepare them for a life ready for nearly any desired opportunity.

One holiday season, on my own, I decided that we were going to do a holiday toy drive for the children of Bankhead Homes. I had no authority or special calling. I was a mid-level, multi-unit HR manager when I walked over to the distribution center and asked for an empty deep freezer box. I wrapped it in colorful wrapping paper. Then I put a sign on it, put up posters and put memos on people's desks. (Yep, this was before email even existed broadly.) Presto! We had a toy drive.

It was so heartwarming to watch it fill up immediately with amazing toys. People also wrote checks or gave me gift cards to shop for them. I was more than happy to help them out, as I can't imagine anything more fun than shopping for toys for needy kids for Christmas. They didn't know how much fun they were losing out on by outsourcing their shopping responsibilities to me.

GOOD COMPANY (IES)

Nonprofit development staff and pastors know that the number one reason people do not give to worthy causes is that they are not asked. If asked, people almost always respond and usually generously. (The next secret is to thank them profusely and authentically so they will give again when asked.) After less than a week, I had a car full of toys for the children of Bankhead Homes, although my plan went slightly askew because I did not research an actual contact person. Instead, I filled up my white Lexus sedan and drove over looking for a community center or someone who could tell me where to best donate them.

I'm not sure exactly what I looked like, driving slowly through Bankhead homes looking to the left and right for someone when I pulled up to two gentlemen whom I assessed to be nice guys and told them what I was doing. They shook their heads at my naivete and told me to stay right there and not drive one foot further. Meanwhile, back at the office, my administrative assistant, Ernie New, told several people that I had taken it upon myself to load up the car and drive over to Bankhead Homes to find a place to donate the toys, so a search party set out to find me as well. What a sitcom I created that day!

While one nice man stayed with me as the other set out to find the de facto "mayor of Bankhead Homes," a matriarch who looked like nobody with whom to mess around. She unlocked the community center as she shook her head at me and my car full of toys. We were all happily unloading the car when the search party from Circuit City's regional office arrived. They helped us finish wrapping the gifts and setting up tables for a Santa Shop that they didn't know they were having the next day. I still think about how much joy that freezer box full of toys brought and not just to the children. The group of us, from different races, ages, and socio-economic backgrounds, working together in a rundown community center to make Christmas a little better for kids. Seeds were definitely planted that day.

My heart was nearly bursting with joy as I drove back to work. I could not even process the lecture on my foolishness and lack of safety that was being recited into my ear by the overly protective coworker who insisted on riding back to work the half-mile through Bankhead Homes. While my plan was perhaps poorly devised, it was pure in motive and most of the people who lived in Bankhead Homes were good people. The odds that I was going to run into good people were in my favor. Bankhead Homes is no longer in existence but there are lots of places in need of Santa Shops and food drives. What's stopping you?

GOOD COMPANY (IES)

Luckily, I did not know about "White Savior Complex" at the time or I might not have done the toy drive, lest I be accused of it. I might have just written a check to the Salvation Army or Toys for Tots not knowing if they delivered to Bankhead Homes. But even in hindsight, I don't think that would have been the better course.

Would the experience have been nearly as lasting or impactful had I just stroked a check and then continued my holiday shopping list? Likely not. I wasn't feeling like I was saving anyone or that I was better than anyone. I felt like I was being a better neighbor by collecting toys from people who had a little extra to give away at the holidays and giving it to those that needed a little extra. Voluntary socialism in its earliest form.

THE IMPORTANCE OF YOUR OWN SEARCH PARTY

The other big point of this story is the search party. The people that you work with are everything. When you change bosses or your boss leaves, it is the equivalent of changing companies. Same thing when your WBF (work best friend) leaves. Your actual job, salary and benefits are important, but you spend so much time at work that the intangibles are very important, including peers, bosses and mentors.

Humbled on Purpose

Everyone needs a search party who will come looking for them whether the danger is real or perceived.

I have been radically blessed by amazing bosses, mentors, peers and friends. I've also been so lucky to have great WBFs at nearly every job I've ever had. As I said at Macy's I had Betsy and Carolyn. At Belk, I had Trish LeDuc, thank goodness! At Circuit City, I had Cindy Batey and Debbie Sharp, we were the three amigos and we were competitive and close at the same time. At HoneyBaked, I had Jo Ann Herold (and others) and I still have Jo Ann, the reason that I am writing this book and pursuing this dream.

Work besties are the best, until you get to the very top. It's hard to have a WBF when you are the CEO or President. When they say it is lonely at the top, they are not lying or even exaggerating. It is. You can't whine too often to your board. You also need to be the optimistic leader to your team. So you need to have an external support team as you really have no internal peers. It's a high class problem—I get that for sure—but it's also real.

I've recently completed hours and hours of coursework to get my certification in executive and leadership coaching. I remember how lonely it can be in the C-suite and I think that I might be able, in my next chapter, to help some C-suite executives as a coach, to feel a little less alone, especially having been there myself.

We spend too much time at work to be lonely or unhappy. We definitely should not spend one minute anywhere that is actually toxic, however, it does make me laugh at how different the definition of what is toxic today in 2024 versus what was typical in the late 1980s when I entered the workforce.

Recently, former Fox News personality Megyn Kelly talked about being asked to 'twirl" for Roger Ailes and how mortified she was when she did it. I won't name the person, but I was asked to "turn around" and show a male senior executive of *human resources* at Macy's my entire outfit, on the sidewalk outside Macy's on Peachtree. However, I was so naive that I didn't even know enough to be mortified. I was flattered that he wanted to see my cute new suit that I had bought, at Macy's, for my interview.

We were in the fashion industry so it really didn't faze me. How times have changed! I was stupid and he was wrong. Even today, though, I don't think I would file a complaint. I'd just say no and move on with the conversation.

There have certainly been other examples, beyond the shoe show incident and being asked to twirl, of toxic situations and hostile workplaces that I have been exposed to in my thirty-plus year career. By and large, though, like my entire life, adversity has made me who I am and has made me a stronger leader, as well as a more confident and capable human.

We always have the choice on how to respond to trouble. We can wallow in victimhood or we can use it to propel us to take a victory lap. I personally love a good victory lap.

CHAPTER 10

THE BIG PICTURE

I THINK everyone should write a book when they turn sixty, even if they never publish it. It is such a great reflective exercise and it is a great memory enhancement. I've spent a considerable amount of time thinking about what my life would be like if I had taken the other job that "Mike" the recruiter offered that day in 2016, the one with the seven-figure annual package with the tough commute and the rough and tumble corporate culture.

I'd probably have a bigger lake house, or at least a big, two-level fancy dock at our current lake house. Sorry boys.

We might even have a place down on 30-A or maybe a place "up north" in Michigan. But does anyone **really** need three houses? We'd probably have gone on a few more extravagant vacations and our retirement accounts would be heftier but we are hardly deprived, (although my kids might write a different version of this chapter). For example, they haven't yet been to Europe which makes them an anomaly in our area. Oh well. They will get that passport stamp soon enough but for now, they will just have to live with Mexico and ski trips. My only real regret is that we would have been able to be so much more generous with the causes that touch our hearts.

When I look back over the last eight years at the CDA, not just the occupation but my whole existence, these have been some of the most joy-filled of my entire life. I have zero regrets. I have been fully present for my sons' high school and college experiences. I have returned to tennis with teams and trips and relationships I cherish. I have gotten my health back under control in a meaningful way. I have invested in my friends with more time than I used to believe I was able to do. Wine Wednesdays with Amy, Debbie, Laurel and Dana is time I treasure. Reconnecting with my besties Lynn and Kari from high school has been priceless. I've been a better wife and family member. I've rediscovered the joy of my women's fraternity Chi Omega and the joy of pouring into this powerful new generation of women coming into the workplace. I have returned to my faith as the center of my life in a more meaningful way than ever before. I am giving back to my alma mater.

When I made the decision in Mike the recruiter's office to go with the "smaller" job, I was taking a road that was abnormal for me. I was largely stepping out on faith rather than trying to control and maximize every dollar that I could earn before I retired. I trusted that God would provide if I used my leadership and talent for something that I felt truly called to do. He has provided.

But the biggest difference that has happened over the past eight years, is that I no longer believe that I took the "little" job, at all. In fact, I am quite certain that I made a much bigger difference in the world over the last eight years by what I have done at the Children's Development Academy than I ever could have done in any corporate role. I might have stored my crowns in heaven but I have also had a much richer life.

If you do the simple math that on average the CDA touches well over 200 children annually plus families and siblings, then I have been involved with making a difference for at least 1,600 children who will have opportunities to excel in kindergarten, high school and life. In turn, these children should not need a CDA for their children, nor should their children, nor their children's children and so on. Breaking generational poverty is not easy nor straightforward, but the most proven way to tackle this systemic problem is to invest in our children with dollars and effort.

We can't help every child, or every needy person in the world, but we don't need to help everyone. We can make an incredible difference by helping the person in front of us. By doing for one, what we wish we could do for many, we start down the path of making a difference. As more of us adopt this practice, more people will be helped and able, in turn, to help others. I think that this is what might ultimately change the world, one child at a time.

When I said no to the seven-figure package and fought for the opportunity to lead the Children's Development Academy, I believe that I said yes to a bigger plan. I am continuing to move forward on that faith even as I write and publish this book, tell my story and speak about the importance of high quality early education, advocate for women in leadership, and better mental health care.

These leaps of faith extend to other business practices like budgeting and planning. I don't always know at the beginning of every fiscal year how we are going to balance the following year's budget, but we always do and we've accumulated nearly a million dollars in reserves, which enabled us to give our teachers those best-in-class raises.

Some of my former colleagues, like Cindy Sutton, whom I have recruited to serve on the CDA board from my "retail is detail" days, barely recognize me as the hands-off, empowering leader as I built the culture I wanted to create at the CDA. I did not know a lot about childcare and did not care to become the resident expert. I had an administrative expert who was good at that side of her job. She recently left and I was able to recruit another expert. I very much focused on strategy, board relations and fundraising. I left the details to the subject matter experts and managers. It worked and it continues to work.

Our faith partners at the CDA are so important to us as volunteers, donors and emotional support. From my literal first day at the CDA, North Point Church has had my back and been a constant source of faith support to me personally. Roswell Presbyterian has also been an amazing partner as has Zion Missionary Baptist been an important partner to the CDA and to me. Personally, I am happy to be home at St. David's Episcopal church, a church that is in the process of getting more involved as a faith partner with the CDA as well. I am no longer a faith-seeking nomad wandering in the proverbial faith desert. I think that having these faith partners, including Cy Mallard, ultimately led me home.

But also in writing this book, it has become more clear to me than ever that I have never been alone in my faith. Even when I was a little girl and felt so very lonely and unloved at times, God was with me and He had big plans for me and my life. The trauma that I went through would pay dividends to generations of children. In my teen years when I was so ashamed of my birth mother's cause of death, I had no idea that I would someday be boldly telling my story of surviving suicide loss, inspiring others to hold on for just one more day and be assured that it does get better. God was even with me when I was rejected by the girls at Hope College and loved so well by my sisters at the Chi Omega at 1525 Washtenaw Avenue in Ann Arbor, and now pouring into and mentoring a new generation of sisters. God was with me when Dr. Doom and Gloom told us that we would not have children and when Riley and Brady were born perhaps to inspire those who struggle with infertility.

I spoke once to a business group in Kennesaw, Georgia, and I told a shortened version of my story. I talked about how, to the outside world it appeared that I had everything, when I was really a broken individual until God revealed his plan for my life to me and gave me the courage to share my story. After the speech, I was approached by Ron Sumpter, the Director of Community Affairs at Cobb EMC, a well respected member of the Cobb County community and a minister. He said that as he drove to the event he felt a message from God in his heart that someone needed to be told to let their light shine. He felt certain after I spoke that this message was meant for me and that I needed to continue to share my story. It took me ten years, but I'm finally ready to do just that. Thanks Ron.

As I wrap up my story, I want to encourage others out there, regardless of where you are on your life's journey; beginning, middle or starting a new chapter, to be bold, even as we are humble. One of my favorite passages that I especially love to share with young women is from Marianne Williamson, "A Return to Love: Reflections on the Principles of "A Course in Miracles." I have this entire passage framed and hanging in my study, but the gist of it says, "Our deepest fear is not that we are inadequate. Our deepest fear is that we are powerful beyond measure. It is our light, not our darkness that most frightens us."

I believe this to be true with everything within me. Especially women, taught as little girls to be afraid to shine, to be too bright, too fast, too anything. I know that I was definitely made to feel ashamed at times if I was ever too proud of myself, reminded that I was not the smartest, the best at

Humbled on Purpose

anything by the world around me.

I read another great quote that said that women and girls don't actually suffer from a lack of confidence, they suffer from an *excess of experience* in how the world deals with confident girls and women. Amen to that!

Even now, I confess that I still feel angst over who am I to write a book, who am I to speak and tell my story, even if it might help someone else, another young woman, perhaps? I might feel angst but I am not going to act on that feeling. God wants us to shine for Him so that others can see His reflected glory in all of His followers and creation. He wants us to help one another and to love one another. I am going to boldly share my scars so that others can feel better about theirs.

But I am now clear that we don't do that by taking the job with the better office, the biggest paycheck, or the nicest view. We do that by making a difference in the biggest way that we can, with as much of our time, our talent and our treasure, as we can, starting as soon as we can.

When I turned down the seven-figure job in 2016, I chose to be humbled on purpose. In that moment, though, I believe that God humbled me *for* purpose as well.

EPILOGUE

THANK YOU for investing the time to read to the end of my book. Time is an abundant, yet also a finite and priceless, gift. I hope (yes, humbly) you find a return on the investment that you gifted to me by reading *Humbled on Purpose*.

Whether you purchased the book or were gifted the hardcopy, e-book, paperback or audiobook, I appreciate that investment, as well. So stay with me while I practice one of my most heartfelt tenets, expressing radical gratitude that I feel to everyone that invests their time and treasure in being part of my *Humbled on Purpose* journey. Thank you!

And now, a quick update: I have left the Children's Development Academy (CDA) in the very capable hands of my successor, CEO and Executive Director, Sheila Sillitto. I'm very proud of the position in which I leave the CDA organizationally, financially and culturally.

As for me, I wrote this book to help launch a new chapter, a third career, if you will, where I write, speak consult, and coach. I want to raise my voice to speak about issues that are important to me, such as high-quality early education for *all* children, especially those from low-income households who are at risk for starting kindergarten ill-prepared.

I also want to speak about women in leadership and keeping women in the workforce so that more women can make it to the C-suite and serve on boards. I hope to talk about raising girls with more confidence to become women in leadership. I plan to make a difference by talking about the importance of mental health and why we should cover it as a medical condition for everyone in their insurance policies.

The proceeds of this book, including speeches and revenue that it generates both direct and ancillary are enabling a matching gift by Bob and I to help fund growth at the CDA. If you wish to donate to the work of the CDA, you can join us at cdakids.org/donate. Choose Humbled on Purpose from the dropdown box so that we can track your gifts and we can thank you personally and radically for joining our cause.

If you'd like to follow me on social media, read my blogs and/or receive my newsletter, all of that can be found at maggiedecan.com. It's a lot like my book; irreverent yet, hopefully, helpful and full of life lessons with more than a touch of God's grace.

EPILOGUE

Thanks again for being part of my story and my next chapter. Let me know if I can help you navigate your next chapter at maggie@maggiedecan.com or connect through my website.

With Grace and Humor,

Maggie

EXPRESSIONS OF RADICAL GRATITUDE

WHERE do I begin to thank everyone who has had a hand in making this dream come true? Well, I'm going to start by apologizing for the people who might look for their name on these pages and not find it. I am so sorry. If you aren't here, it doesn't mean that I'm not wildly grateful, but I had to do this on a short deadline. I wish I had more time to marinade and ponder. I know the minute that I press send, I am going to think of 5 more people that I should have thanked. Please know how grateful I am to everyone that has encouraged me along the way, known and called out here and those whose crowns are stored in heaven.

While I dedicated the book to them, thanks again to my immediate family. You were supportive with my time and energy drain as well as letting me expose some warts in the book.

Bob—You have loved me well, first as my best friend in ninth grade and then as my everything forever. You have been my roots and my wings even when I am not easy. Thank you for every day of being there. I love you.

Riley—We thank God for the miracle of you and for making us a family. Thank you for showing me what unconditional love is when it entered my heart for you. Someday you will understand how much we love you and how much you changed our lives. We love you and Emily so much, to the moon and back.

Brady—You miraculously completed our family and grew my heart in a way that I did not know that I could love. You are an amazing brother, friend and son. I cannot imagine the world without you in it. You are our miracle child that we could not even dream of holding. You are my sunshine.

I also need to thank my extended family—Mom, Nancy, Dan, Ben, and Deb—for allowing me to open some family closets. I love you all. Even members of my family who are no longer here to defend their names and might not come across well in the book, are still beloved by me and helped shape me for the better. I love you Dad and Mom.

Thank you to Jo Ann Streiff Herold, MBA, ACC, CMO, WBF,

EXPRESSIONS OF RADICAL GRATITUDE

author, speaker and mentor extraordinaire. You changed my life at the Canyon Ranch. Thank you, partner!

To my "launch team" that has been asking how to help since they heard about my book, through title changes and all. Your belief in me gave me confidence, thank you for lifting me up and helping me not doubt myself because you did not doubt me! Thank you Allison Stephanouk, you are so much more than a tennis friend. You are a true friend, a web genius, and an amazing person. You saved my bum! I owe you some Finnish cocktails and more.

My wine Wednesday "civic group," Dana, Laurel, Amy, Debbie, you are my rocks. All my Roswell friends, my so much more than just tennis friends, my neighbors, my RNE, CMS, RHS, baseball friends, my CDA friends, my Spring Lake friends (Lynn, Kari, Toni), my more than just social media friends; I am so blessed by you all. Thank you for buying (and reading) my book. (Now please, don't forget to review it on Amazon and Goodreads! Sorry, am I never satisfied?)

Thanks to my HoneyBaked Ham, Circuit City, Belk, and Macy's family, all of you made me better even when I was perfectly awful. And the mentors that I have been so blessed to have; Chuck Bengochea, Mark Arensmeyer, Pete Douglas, Mike Froning, Bill Zierden, Pat Pinardo, Bill Brigham, the late Russ Grunewald, Tim Belk, Doug Higgins, Joseph Alonso, Ron Hancock and so many others who've touched my career. Even those on whom I practiced bad management on until I became a more vulnerable, better leader. Thank you!

Thank you to the CDA boards of eight years and the staff team that put up with the corporate refugee in 2016 and supported me so lovingly this past year. Thank you to my "favorite" Marcia. Thank you Chris/MacGyver. Thank you Sheila, Donna, and team. Thank you to Lisa for calling from Alaska. Thank you for joining us Cassidy and for sticking with us Yehymmy, Kathy, Judith, and Erinn. Thanks for all you gave us Marla. Thanks to all the teachers who do the hardest jobs of all with love and dedication for far less money than they deserve, still.

Speaking of teachers, thank you to Mr. Wolbrink. You were right. Maggie Michaels is the name of an author! I am a writer. You planted the seed as great teachers do. Thank you so much. Great teachers, like Bob, are worth their weight in gold. As are you.

To the North Fulton faith and civic community family, my beloved church home—St. David's Episcopal church, Roswell Presbyterian, North Point Community Church, Zion Missionary Baptist Church, Roswell Baptist Church, and so many others that support the CDA. Thank you to the Rotarians, Roswell Women's Clubs, Junior Leagues, NCLs, YMSLs, Kiwanis, Lions, Optimists, Eagles Scouts, Girls Scouts, schools and so many others. Thank you for your support the last eight years and for the next eighty! I know you will be there for CDA's kids.

To my nonprofit "sisters" Gail, Rose, Kathy, Barbara, Nancy, Andrea, Cheryl, Stephanie and Joe (okay brother Joe) so many others who helped me when I was just learning? I hope we never have to find out what communities look like without nonprofit safety nets for our most vulnerable.

Thanks to my Chi O sisters, Etas from Ann Arbor, my Atlanta bunch, Nancy Walton Laurie cohort sisters (Julie Andrews misses you and yes KM is gone), my pearls; Emily Armour, Lainie Lawrence, Gemma Schonken, and Rachel Woods! Thank you to my friends who do so much to protect our Fraternity; Erin Packwood, Letitia Fulkerson, Sally Kimball, Leslie Herington, Ann Bradshaw, Kelly Bingel, Susan Miller Bush, Marcia MacLeod, Leslee Budge, Danna Redmond, Cathey Humphreys, Jan Heck, Corrina Casey, Elaine Baker, Stephanie Olmsted, Sarah Vogel and the incomparable Laura Miller. Thank you for finding me Heather! I keep you all ever at heart and you inspire me. Chi Omega gave me a family and belonging when I needed it so! XOXO LICO

Humbled on Purpose

To my aMAIZING University of Michigan brethren in Michigan, Atlanta and beyond, Go Blue! Thanks for such an inspiring 2023, especially to team 144 and all who follow! Who's got it better than us? Nobody! We got the Natty. Now we are getting that Georgia License plate!

To Ripples Media for making this dream come true, thank you. Thank you Jeff Hilimire, for creating a company to tell positive stories that might make a difference and spread positive ripples out into the world. You are a dreamweaver. Thank you Nicole Wedekind for coming in the nick of time to help me launch. Thank you to all the authors who helped with the text accountability and brainstorming, especially Adam Albrecht, who has been inspiring me since I "got quit" in 2016. Thank you to Burtch Hunter for my amazing cover design and the Matherly family for their clutch assist.

Considering writing a book? I'd love to tell you more about it, email me at maggie@maggiedecan.com.

Thank you to my amazing editor Andrew Vogel for believing in me, my writing, and my story from the first time we Zoomed and laughed so much. Thank you for encouraging me to tell it all, recognizing imposter syndrome, forcing me to be brave and giving me confidence. I wrote a better book because of you. I wrote the book God meant for me to write because of you.

Most of all, thanks be to God.

ABOUT THE AUTHOR

MAGGIE DeCAN stepped down in the fall of 2024 as the CEO & Executive Director of the Children's Development Academy (CDA), a 501(c)3 providing high-quality early education to children from low income families to publish her first book, *Humbled on Purpose*. She also focuses on speaking, coaching, consulting, and writing about early education, women in leadership and mental health.

Before leading the CDA, DeCan was the President & Chief Operating Officer at The HoneyBaked Ham Company, LLC, where she led 500 stores, ecommerce and over $500 million in annual revenue. Prior to HoneyBaked, she held operational and HR leadership roles at Circuit City, Belk, and Macy's.

Known for a leadership style of serving those who serve the customers, she has been recognized by the National Diversity Council, as a most powerful woman. She has also been awarded the P.O.W. award by Womenetics, with the Turknett Character in Leadership Award and The Georgia PTA for Visionary Leadership.

When not writing or playing tennis with the Atlanta Lawn Tennis Association (ALTA) or USTA, Maggie volunteers with the Chi Omega National Fraternity Foundation and as a mentor to collegians, serves as president of the Atlanta University of Michigan Alumni Club and serves her parish at St. David's Episcopal Church as a Lay Eucharistic Minister and Lector.

Maggie and her husband Bob live in Woodstock, Georgia. They have two sons, Riley and Brady, along with their new daughter-in-law Emily. They also enjoy time at their home on Lake Nottely in the north Georgia mountains with their labs Charlie and Lily.

PASS HUMBLED ON

STOP! Please don't put *Humbled on Purpose* on your bookshelf. It was written to help people. *Pass Humbled on.*

Write an encouraging note to someone, stick it inside and share the book. *Pass Humbled on.*

Put it in a Little Free Library or give it to a friend. *Pass Humbled on.*

Don't make Humbled part of your dusty library. Give Humbled away, please. *Pass Humbled on.*

Post a note on social media about the lessons you learned or who you are helping. You can help me by going to Amazon or Barnes & Noble to give my first book a great review. Then maybe even stop by Goodreads! *Pass Humbled on.*

Email me (maggie@maggiedecan.com). I'd love to know that I helped you, even a little. I'd love to know that you are helping someone else.

Thank you, from the bottom of this author's radically grateful, healing heart.

Maggie

Printed in the USA
CPSIA information can be obtained
at www.ICGtesting.com
LVHW062226021224
798162LV00012B/49